HIKING ARIZONA

by

DON R. KIEFER

Golden West Publishers

Front and back covers designed by Bruce Fischer / The Book Studio

All maps drawn by J. L. Abernathy-Gilbert

CAUTION

Physical hazards may be encountered in visiting areas of *Hiking Arizona*, particularly old mining localities. Land ownerships and road conditions change over the years. Readers should take proper precautions and make local inquiries, as author and publishers cannot accept responsibility for such matters. Ranger districts are identified to facilitate obtaining the most current information about specific trails.

Library of Congress Cataloging-in-Publication Data

Kiefer, Don
    Hiking Arizona / by Don Kiefer.
    Includes index.
    1. Hiking--Arizona--Guide-books. 2. Arizona--Description and travel--Guide-books.   I. Title.
GV199.42.A7K54 1991   91-4512
917.91'0433--dc20   CIP
ISBN 0-914846-54-X

Printed in the United States of America

Information in this book is deemed to be authentic and accurate by authors and publisher. However, they disclaim any liability incurred in connection with the use of information appearing in this book.

Golden West Publishers   **(602) 265-4392**
4113 N. Longview Ave.
Phoenix, AZ 85014, USA

Dedication

I dedicate this book to my son,
Monte A. Kiefer,
who has chosen to start his adult life
in the breathtaking Smoky Mountains of North Carolina.
It is my way of allowing him to spend time with me,
through this book,
though many miles stretch between us.

Acknowledgements

Few books are written and prepared for publication by only one person. This book is no exception. Many people and organizations spent time and effort to make this book a success.

My thanks to:

Evelyn Long, of Gilbert, Arizona, has for five years taken my rough drafts and prepared them into something worth printing.

Mesa Tribune, Mesa, Arizona, gave me the liberty of publishing my experiences for others to enjoy.

J. L. Abernathy-Gilbert, a special co-worker at Colossal Cave, has put up with some of my crudely scribbled maps, and because of her superb artistic talent, turned them into the works of art you see in this book.

Kenneth Ward, Dick Higdon and *Larry Mutter* have kept me company on many a mile in our wonderful state of Arizona.

Joe Maierhauser, lease owner and manager of Colossal Cave Park, has willingly given me the time and use of his facilities along with his encouragement to make this book become what it is.

Additionally, I would like to thank all of the following for their support and assistance in securing information and consents:

Herman's World of Sporting Goods, Maricopa County Civil Defense & Emergency Services, Springerville Ranger District, Chalender Ranger District, Williams Ranger District, Payson Ranger District, Bob's Bargain Barn, Mesa Ranger District, Santa Catalina Ranger District, Nogales Ranger District, Pleasant Valley Ranger District, Chiricahua National Monument (Richard Frear Photos), Saguaro National Monument East, Arizona State Parks, Maricopa County Parks & Recreation, City of Phoenix Parks, Recreation & Library Department, Arizona Game & Fish.

Again, thanks to all of you for going out of your way for me.

Don R. Kiefer

Contents

Arizona map...inside front cover

Introduction...6

TRAILS

(Letters in front of trail names refer to location on state map.)

(continued on next page)

(contents continued)

Introduction

The Rim Country! Just the mention of its name is inviting, urging one to hike in a place where cares and frustrations don't exist. With its lofty peaks that cast deep shadows and winds that twist through the pines to whisper of years and events of long ago, this is an area that can dwarf a person. Scents surround you, beauty engulfs you, and your ears are filled with sounds uncommon to daily city life — sounds like continuously running creeks, waterfalls and bird calls.

Then there are the Chiricahua Mountains, mountains that have withstood the test of gusting winds, driving rain, chilling cold and searing heat. The result is a wonderland of rock, spires and pinnacles. A visit to the Chiricahuas is like a visit to an unknown planet with columns that tower hundreds of feet above your head amidst carefully-balanced rocks of fantastic shapes.

I could go on about the Santa Ritas, Santa Catalinas, Rincons, Mazatzals, Superstitions, areas of the White Mountains above 11,000 feet, and more. The trails described in *Hiking Arizona* are designed as a guide to hiking the deserts and mountains of Arizona. The state is vast and intimidating to those who do not know where to hike.

All 50 of these trails are special to me in one way or another, no matter how easy or difficult. Each trail chapter is accompanied by description and statistics, plus a map of the trail itself and its surrounding area.

As a reference, the book also includes desert and mountain survival information, as well as guidelines on outfitting for your hike and hiking etiquette, also a list of agencies and how to get in touch with them for detailed information about the trails.

Although great care has been taken creating the maps in this book, I would strongly urge you to purchase topographic maps that correspond to the trails you are taking.

There are three additional maps included in *Hiking Arizona* for your reference: Highline Trail (in the rim country north of Payson), the Rincons and the Chiricahuas, both southeast of Tucson. These reference maps can be used to plan your day, possibly expanding your hike to include side trails, or perhaps a hike from a different direction. In short, these maps will enable you to create an excursion to suit your own wants.

I hope reading *Hiking Arizona* will inspire you and encourage you to experience for yourself!

Don R. Kiefer

WEST FORK TRAIL

Springerville Ranger District — (602) 333-4372

DIRECTION: Trailhead at Sheep Crossing Campground to saddle at 11,000 feet

To reach the trailhead, take Forest Road #87 south out of Greer about six miles to its junction with Forest Road #113, turn left and continue for 2.2 miles to Sheep Crossing Campground and the trail head.

This trail begins near Sheep Crossing and ascends along the west fork of the Little Colorado River. The trail remains on soft, grassy slopes for about two miles before entering the forest.

About five miles from the trailhead, you will come to a ridge leading to the top; it is unmistakable as you look down both sides. In another 1.5 miles, you will come to the junction of the two trails at 11,000 feet. This should serve as your turn-around point.

Please respect the off-limits on the peak, as it is sacred to the Apaches. People have been found on the peak by the Indians only to have a perfect day turn into disaster.

REQUIREMENTS: 6-7 hours hiking time round trip; water, food, raingear, warm clothes

LOCATION: 8 miles southeast of Greer in the White Mountains

DIFFICULTY: Moderate

ELEVATIONS: 9200' to 11,000'

LENGTH: 7 miles one way

MAPS REQUIRED: Mt. Ord Quadrangle; 7.5 minute topographic Apache County

PERMIT: No

WATER: Sometimes West Fork, but not dependable

INFORMATION: Do not continue on the last 403' to the summit — it is sacred Apache land.

ATTRACTION: Fantastic views and breathtaking alpine environment.

WEST FORK
TRAIL

SCALE ⊢————⊣ 1 MILE

NORTH

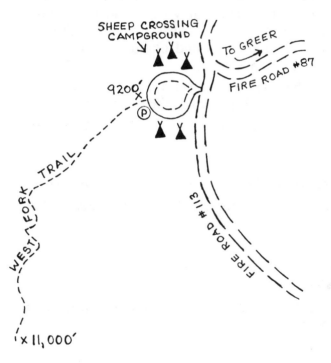

SHEEP CROSSING CAMPGROUND

TO GREER

FIRE ROAD #87

9200' x

Ⓟ

WEST FORK TRAIL

FIRE ROAD #113

x 11,000'

WINTER SPRING SUMMER FALL

SOUTH FORK TRAIL

Springerville Ranger District — (602) 333-4372

DIRECTION: South Fork Campground to three-mile mark on South Fork Trail

South Fork Campground is located seven miles west of Eagar on State Route #260. At this point, turn south on Forest Road #506. This is 2½ miles of good road that takes you to the trailhead at the campground.

This is a very easy trail up to the three-mile mark, with many grassy areas where one can enjoy a picnic lunch and even listen to the tiny waterfalls. The trail skirts South Fork Creek in the entire three miles and the sound of flowing water goes hand-in-hand with the cool shade.

Many times I have sat by the creek's edge and watched the fish on their merry way as I listened to the birds up above.

Do not attempt the rest of this trail unless you are experienced.

REQUIREMENTS: 3 hours hiking time round trip; water, snack

LOCATION: South Fork Campground; Apache-Sitgreaves National Forest, Greer

DIFFICULTY: Easy

ELEVATIONS: 7600′ to 8100′

LENGTH: 3 miles one way

MAPS REQUIRED: Greer Quadrangle; 7.5 minute topographic, Apache County

PERMIT: No

WATER: Year 'round

INFORMATION: Trail is 6 miles long — only maintained for 3 miles.

ATTRACTION: Nice area to fish and enjoy the creek and solitude

SOUTH FORK TRAIL

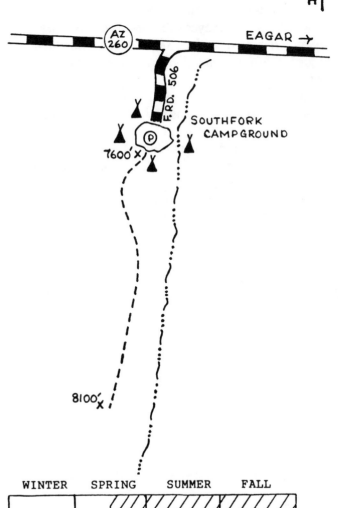

SCALE = 1 MILE

NORTH

AZ 260

EAGAR →

F. RD. 506

SOUTHFORK CAMPGROUND

7600' X

8100' X

WINTER   SPRING   SUMMER   FALL

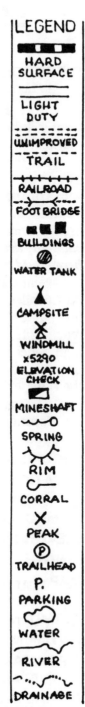

LEGEND

HARD SURFACE

LIGHT DUTY

UNIMPROVED TRAIL

RAILROAD

FOOT BRIDGE

BUILDINGS

WATER TANK

CAMPSITE

WINDMILL

x5290 ELEVATION CHECK

MINESHAFT

SPRING

RIM

CORRAL

PEAK

TRAILHEAD

P. PARKING

WATER

RIVER

DRAINAGE

COCHISE COUNTY

ECHO CANYON TRAIL

Chiricahua National Monument — (602) 824-3560

DIRECTION: Echo Canyon Trailhead to Hailstone Trail and back to Echo Canyon Trailhead via loop

Take Bonita Canyon drive from Chiricahua Visitors Center (about 5½ miles) to trailhead. The turnoff is well marked.

On this spacious trail, you will slowly start to descend. Soon you will find yourself almost able to reach out and touch some of the gigantic spires. At about one mile, you will find yourself in a "Swiss cheese" honeycomb. *Some of the huge arches and bridges have floors that slope downhill, then suddenly drop down 150 feet or more. Failure to move carefully here could be fatal.*

Near the base of Echo Canyon, the trail enters Echo Park. At 1.6 miles, you will come to a fork in the trail. To continue this hike, take the left fork and, a mile beyond Echo Park, you will reach Totem Canyon, where giant rock columns reach 300 feet high. Since your left turn, you have been on Hailstone Trail, and on your left are millions of marble-sized volcanic materials; on the right, excellent views of Rhyolite Canyon.

The trail flows moderately uphill near the end, and again there's another fork in the trail. Take the left fork and, in 1,000 feet, you will be back at the point from where you started.

REQUIREMENTS: 2 hours hiking time round trip; water, food

LOCATION: Chiricahua National Monument, National Park Service.

DIFFICULTY: Easy

ELEVATIONS: 6320' to 6760'

LENGTH: 3.5 miles round trip

MAPS REQUIRED: Cochise Head Quadrangle; 7.5 minute series topographic, Cochise County.

PERMIT: No

WATER: No

INFORMATION: A small fee is charged at Visitors Center— must carry receipt.

ATTRACTION: Spectacular rock formations.

ECHO CANYON
TRAIL

SCALE: |⎿_____⏌| 1 MILE

NORTH

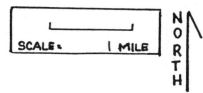

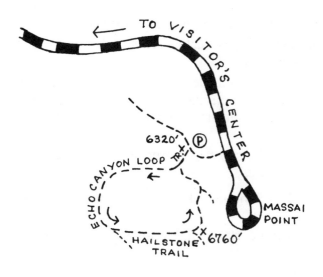

TO VISITOR'S CENTER

6320' (P)

ECHO CANYON LOOP TR.

MASSAI POINT

X 6760'

HAILSTONE TRAIL

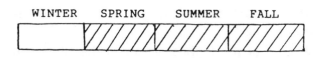

WINTER	SPRING	SUMMER	FALL

LEGEND

▬⬜▬⬜▬ HARD SURFACE

──── LIGHT DUTY

┅┅┅┅ UNIMPROVED
╌╌╌╌ TRAIL

╫╫╫╫ RAILROAD

→‖←‖→ FOOT BRIDGE

■■■ BUILDINGS

⊘ WATER TANK

⛺ CAMPSITE

🌀 WINDMILL

x5290 ELEVATION CHECK

▰ MINESHAFT

⌁o SPRING

⌓ RIM

C CORRAL

X PEAK

(P) TRAILHEAD

P. PARKING

WATER

RIVER

DRAINAGE

SUGARLOAF MOUNTAIN TRAIL

Chiricahua National Monument — (602) 824-3560

DIRECTION: Trailhead at parking lot to peak

From the Visitors Center at Chiricahua National Monument, take Bonita Canyon Road towards Massai Point and, at about 5½ miles, there will be a right-hand turn to the trailhead and parking area just below Sugarloaf Mountain; it is well marked.

The trail beginning here heads to the summit and to a fire lookout constructed there in 1935. The trail climbs gradually and, along the way, passes through a small tunnel.

The last quarter-mile gets a little steeper and there are loose rocks, so watch your footing!

When you have reached the summit, you are sure to be awestruck by the 360° panoramic view of Arizona and New Mexico. Visible are more unusual rock formations than you can imagine.

Be sure to walk the short interpretive trail at the top to learn more about the area.

REQUIREMENTS: 1.5 hours hiking time round trip; water, snack

LOCATION: Chiricahua National Monument, National Park Service

DIFFICULTY: Easy

ELEVATIONS: 6797′ to 7307′

LENGTH: 1 mile one way

MAPS REQUIRED: Cochise Head Quadrangle; 7.5 minute series topographic, Cochise County.

PERMIT: No

WATER: No

INFORMATION: A small fee is charged at Visitors Center — must carry receipt.

ATTRACTION: One of the highest views in the Chiricahua National Monument.

SUGARLOAF MOUNTAIN TRAIL

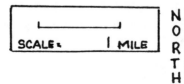

SCALE: 1 MILE

NORTH

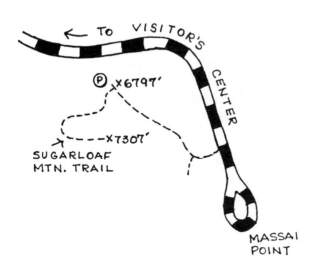

← TO VISITOR'S CENTER

Ⓟ x6797'

x7307'

SUGARLOAF MTN. TRAIL

MASSAI POINT

WINTER   SPRING   SUMMER   FALL

NATURAL BRIDGE TRAIL

Chiricahua National Monument — (602) 824-3560

DIRECTION: Trailhead on Bonita Canyon Drive to the bridge itself

Access to the trailhead is gained by taking the Bonita Canyon Drive from the monument's Visitors Center, which is 1¼ mile from the Natural Bridge parking area.

After climbing to the canyon rim through areas of welcome shade, a rest is in order. Take this time to gaze down Bonita Canyon with your field glasses to appreciate where you are. At 6,080 feet, this is your highest point on the hike.

The trail now drops, via switchbacks, into a dense stand of Arizona cypress called Picket Park. Not far beyond Picket Park, the trail ends just before the end of a small canyon.

The Natural Bridge is just across the deep wash to your left as you reach the trail's end. Prepare to look hard, as trees tend to keep it hidden.

REQUIREMENTS: 4.5 hours hiking time round trip; water, snack, raingear

LOCATION: Picket Park; Chiricahua National Monument, National Park Service

DIFFICULTY: Moderate

ELEVATIONS: 5560' to 6080'

LENGTH: 5 miles round trip

MAPS REQUIRED: Cochise Head Quadrangle; 7.5 minute series topographic, Cochise County.

PERMIT: No

WATER: Not dependable

INFORMATION: A small fee is charged at Visitors Center — must carry receipt.

ATTRACTION: 30' hidden arch; interesting outcropping rock formations.

NATURAL BRIDGE TRAIL

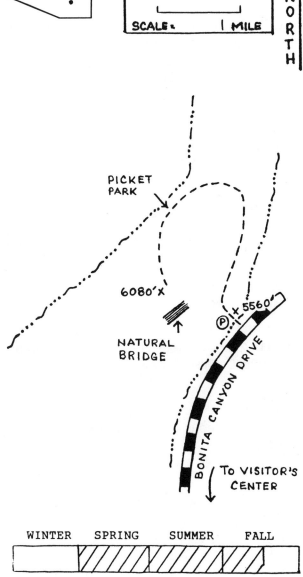

SCALE: |___| 1 MILE

NORTH

PICKET PARK

6080' X

NATURAL BRIDGE

P + 5560'

BONITA CANYON DRIVE

TO VISITOR'S CENTER

WINTER   SPRING   SUMMER   FALL

RHYOLITE CANYON TRAIL

Chiracahua National Monument — (602) 824-3560

DIRECTION: Chiricahua Visitors Center to Heart of Rocks area

The trailhead is right at the edge of the parking lot at the Visitors Center.

The trail is wide, but bear to the right to avoid the short nature trail. The unusual scenery starts almost with your first step, as countless spires appear. The first 1½ miles of trail are very easy going with pleasant views and only 260 feet of altitude gain.

Then you come to a fork in the trail; take the right, as it leads into Sarah Deming Canyon toward the Heart of Rocks, a strenuous climb, gaining almost 1,200 feet in 1½ miles.

See how many formations you can pick out on the one-mile loop trail at the top.

REQUIREMENTS: 3.5 hours hiking time round trip; water, snack

LOCATION: Chiricahua National Monument, National Park Service

DIFFICULTY: Difficult at times

ELEVATIONS: 5400' to 6860'

LENGTH: 3.2 miles one way

MAPS REQUIRED: Cochise Head Quadrangle; 7.5 minute series topographic, Cochise County.

PERMIT: No

WATER: Not in dry season

INFORMATION: A small fee is charged at Visitors Center — must carry receipt.

ATTRACTION: Heart of Rocks formation.

RHYOLITE CANYON TRAIL

SCALE = 1 MILE

NORTH

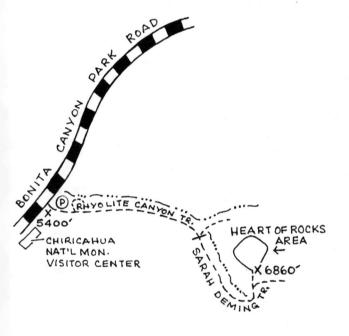

BONITA CANYON PARK ROAD

Ⓟ RHYOLITE CANYON TR.

X 5400'

CHIRICAHUA NAT'L MON. VISITOR CENTER

SARAH DEMING TR.

HEART OF ROCKS AREA ←

X 6860'

WINTER   SPRING   SUMMER   FALL

LEGEND

HARD SURFACE

LIGHT DUTY

UNIMPROVED TRAIL

RAILROAD

FOOT BRIDGE

BUILDINGS

WATER TANK

CAMPSITE

WINDMILL

x5290 ELEVATION CHECK

MINESHAFT

SPRING

RIM

CORRAL

PEAK

Ⓟ TRAILHEAD

P. PARKING

WATER

RIVER

DRAINAGE

COCONINO COUNTY

KENDRICK MOUNTAIN TRAIL

Chalender Ranger District — (602) 635-2676

DIRECTION: Trailhead to peak

From Flagstaff, take I-40 west to the Parks exit (16 miles) and turn right to a T intersection. Turn left and travel 0.4 miles to Spring Valley Road and turn right at the Union 76 station. Take Spring Valley Road eight miles and turn onto Forest Road #194 (well marked). Take #194 about four miles to Forest Road #171 and turn right. Go three miles to Forest Road #171A, turn left and drive one mile to the trailhead.

After crossing through a small gate, the first mile of this trail follows an old road, with wide access and gentle switchbacks, which, in just over a mile, turns into a spacious trail.

The trail is constantly uphill, clear to the top, through thinned-out ponderosa pine, Douglas fir, white fir, southwest white pine and corkbark fir.

Be sure to stop and take in the views, such as more cinder cones from volcanic activity than you can count, along with views of the Grand Canyon and Painted Desert.

At the 10,000-foot level, you will be confronted with a grassy area with a view that seems to go on forever, and also an old fire-watch cabin. From here it is only a quarter-mile to the peak and the firetower.

REQUIREMENTS: 5-6 hours hiking time round trip; water, warm clothes, raingear, food

LOCATION: Kaibab National Forest; 16 miles west of Flagstaff

DIFFICULTY: Moderate

ELEVATIONS: 7980′ to 10418′

LENGTH: 3.5 miles one way

MAPS REQUIRED: Kendrick Peak Quadrangle; 7.5 minute series topographic, Coconino County.

PERMIT: No

WATER: No

INFORMATION: Severe storms develop quickly at this altitude

ATTRACTION: Views of Grand Canyon, Painted Desert, Snow Bowl and Sunset Crater

KENDRICK MOUNTAIN TRAIL

SCALE = 1 MILE

NORTH

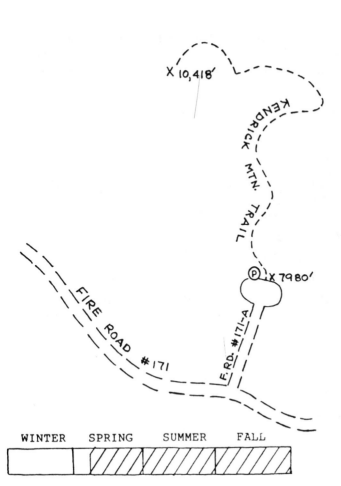

X 10,418'

KENDRICK MTN. TRAIL

P ⊙ X 7980'

F.R.D. #171-A

FIRE ROAD #171

WINTER	SPRING	SUMMER	FALL

LEGEND

HARD SURFACE

LIGHT DUTY

UNIMPROVED TRAIL

RAILROAD

FOOT BRIDGE

BUILDINGS

WATER TANK

CAMPSITE

WINDMILL

x5290 ELEVATION CHECK

MINESHAFT

SPRING

RIM

CORRAL

PEAK

TRAILHEAD

P. PARKING

WATER

RIVER

DRAINAGE

BILL WILLIAMS TRAIL

Williams Ranger District — (602) 635-2633

DIRECTION: Trailhead at Ranger Station to peak

In Williams, go west on Bill Williams Avenue about one mile, turn left at Clover Hill and proceed along the frontage road to the turnoff to Williams Ranger District Office. Follow the signs to the trailhead.

The trail starts out easy. As you cross West Cataract Creek, it goes through aspens and ferns. Several points along the trail offer good views of the valley below and distant peaks.

Although the trail is well kept, the forest still closes in on you with some of the largest aspen I have ever seen. Up further, the winds begin to increase as the last tenth of the hike gets a little steep.

Three miles from the start the trail terminates at a gravel road that winds to the top of the mountain. From the top, breathtaking views await you.

REQUIREMENTS: 4-5 hours hiking time round trip; water, food, warm clothes, raingear

LOCATION: 1 mile west of Williams

DIFFICULTY: Moderate

ELEVATIONS: 7000' to 9256'

LENGTH: 3.5 miles one way

MAPS REQUIRED: Bill Williams Mtn. 15 min. USGS Quadrangle; Kaibab National Forest South Map, Coconino County.

PERMIT: No

WATER: No

INFORMATION: Violent storms and high winds develop quickly on peak.

ATTRACTION: A toll was charged around 1902 for the view from the top. Now it's free.

BILL WILLIAMS TRAIL

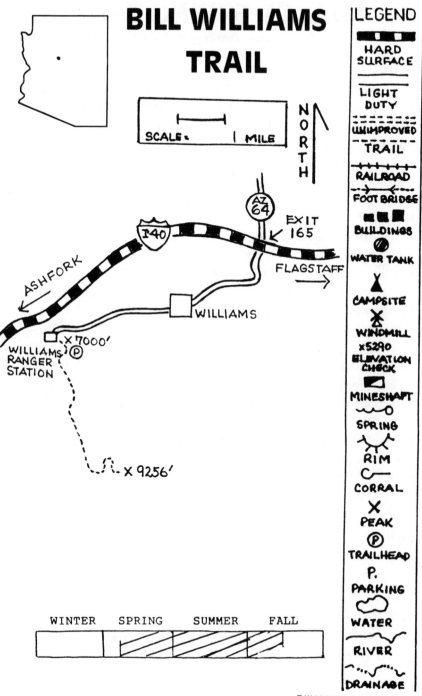

SCALE = 1 MILE

NORTH

AZ 64

EXIT 165

I-40

FLAGSTAFF →

ASHFORK

WILLIAMS

× 7000'

WILLIAMS RANGER STATION

P

× 9256'

WINTER   SPRING   SUMMER   FALL

LEGEND

HARD SURFACE

LIGHT DUTY

UNIMPROVED

TRAIL

RAILROAD

FOOT BRIDGE

BUILDINGS

WATER TANK

CAMPSITE

WINDMILL

×5290 ELEVATION CHECK

MINESHAFT

SPRING

RIM

CORRAL

× PEAK

P TRAILHEAD

P. PARKING

WATER

RIVER

DRAINAGE

TURKEY SPRING TRAIL

Payson Ranger District — (602) 474-2269

DIRECTION: Geronimo to top of Milk Ranch Point

From intersection of SR 87 and Control Road, proceed east on Control Road 5 miles to Camp Geronimo turnoff, then 2 miles to camp parking lot. (A map at the camp entrance indicates proper path of trail through camp.)

The trail through Camp Geronimo is .7 mile. At .9 mile, the trail splits with Turkey Spring Trail to the right. When you reach the 1.3 mile mark, there is a sharp left hairpin turn that is easy to miss if one isn't careful.

Mile mark 1.5 brings you to the back end of Turkey Spring and it is here that the trail leaves an old road and heads straight uphill to the rim via a natural drainage trough.

A natural rock formation called Balanced Rock appears on the left at mile mark 2.25. From Balanced Rock, a series of long switchbacks brings you to mile mark 2.6 and the rim.

There is only .4 mile to FR 218 from the point where the trail tops the rim, bringing the total trail length to 3 miles.

Other trails that are accessed from Milk Ranch Point are: The Rim Road (FR 300), West Webber, Milk Ranch Point West, and Donahue.

REQUIREMENTS: 2 hours hiking time one way; water, snack, raingear

LOCATION: NW out of Camp Geronimo, Tonto Nat. Forest

DIFFICULTY: Easy to moderate

ELEVATIONS: 5600′ to 7220′

LENGTH: 3 miles one way

MAPS REQUIRED: Pine Quadrangle; 7.5 minute series topographic, Gila County.

PERMIT: No

WATER: Not dependable

INFORMATION: Summer storms develop quickly

ATTRACTION: Shortest route to top of Milk Ranch from Camp Geronimo.

TURKEY SPRING TRAIL

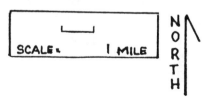

SCALE: 1 MILE

NORTH

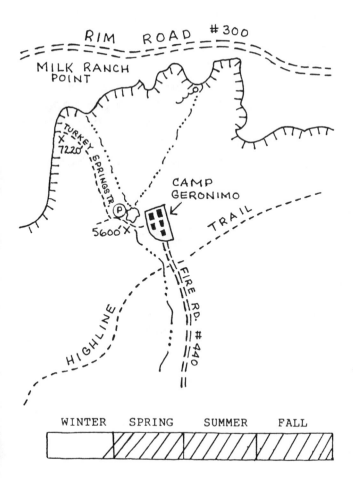

RIM ROAD #300

MILK RANCH POINT

TURKEY SPRINGS TR.

X 7220

CAMP GERONIMO

5600' X

P

TRAIL

HIGHLINE

FIRE RD. #440

WINTER	SPRING	SUMMER	FALL

LEGEND

HARD SURFACE

LIGHT DUTY

UNIMPROVED

TRAIL

RAILROAD

FOOT BRIDGE

BUILDINGS

WATER TANK

CAMPSITE

WINDMILL

x5290
ELEVATION CHECK

MINESHAFT

SPRING

RIM

CORRAL

PEAK

P TRAILHEAD

P. PARKING

WATER

RIVER

DRAINAGE

SEE CANYON TRAIL

Payson Ranger District — (602) 474-2269

DIRECTION: Forest Rd. #300 South to Highline Trail #31

Access to See Canyon trailhead is gained by taking State Route 260 east out of Payson for 28 miles where a left turn is made onto Forest Road #300. This is a gravel road but is fit for automobiles. After leaving Route 260, watch for trailhead sign in 12.3 miles on left side of road.

At the start of this breathtaking trail, a beauty develops around you that does not exist on any other trail in the system. You will be especially taken in by the many flowing tributaries the trail crosses. Also, there is the smell of clean, fresh air, not to mention the lush greenery, including the moss on the live and dead trees as well as on the rocks. Makes you feel as if you have visited an area that time has forgotten.

About one-half mile from the intersection with Highline Trail #31 is a spur trail on the left leading to See Spring, approximately one-half mile in length. The water seeps from the ground under the very rocks on which you walk.

The real beauty is in the See Canyon Trail itself. It is a most inspiring trail!

REQUIREMENTS: 3 hours hiking time one way; water, food, raingear

LOCATION: West of Woods Canyon Lake, Tonto National Forest

DIFFICULTY: Moderate

ELEVATIONS: 7880′ to 5894′

LENGTH: 4.1 miles one way

MAPS REQUIRED: Promontory Butte Quadrangle; 7.5 minute series topographic, Gila County

PERMIT: No

WATER: Not dependable

INFORMATION: Don't forget camera here; summer storms gather quickly

ATTRACTION: Breathtaking scenery

SEE CANYON TRAIL

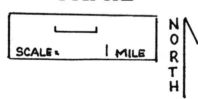

SCALE = 1 MILE

NORTH

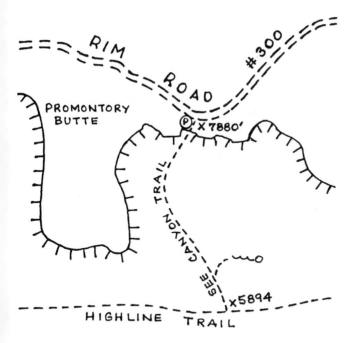

RIM ROAD #300

PROMONTORY BUTTE

P X 7880'

SEE CANYON TRAIL

X 5894

HIGHLINE TRAIL

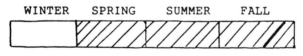

WINTER	SPRING	SUMMER	FALL

LEGEND

HARD SURFACE

LIGHT DUTY

UNIMPROVED TRAIL

RAILROAD

FOOT BRIDGE

BUILDINGS

WATER TANK

CAMPSITE

WINDMILL

x5290 ELEVATION CHECK

MINESHAFT

SPRING

RIM

CORRAL

PEAK

Ⓟ TRAILHEAD

P. PARKING

WATER

RIVER

DRAINAGE

MYRTLE TRAIL

Payson Ranger District — (602) 474-2269

DIRECTION: From trailhead on Forest Road #300 at a point 33 miles northwest of Highway 260 to the intersection with Highline Trail #31

At the trailhead, a good sign gives directions. The going is easy as you pass through a gate at .10 mile. At .20 mile, the second gate is encountered, at which point the trail begins its descent. It is easy to follow and easy to travel.

At its termination with Highline Trail #31, a right turn onto Highline will take you to Washington Park in 9.50 miles.

A left turn onto Highline takes you to a point on Forest Road #289 just below the Fish Hatchery parking lot, a distance of 7.2 miles.

REQUIREMENTS: 1 hour hiking time one way; water, snack, raingear

LOCATION: 33 miles Northwest of Arizona Route 260 on Rim Road; Tonto National Forest

DIFFICULTY: Easy

ELEVATIONS: 7824' to 6800'

LENGTH: 1.5 miles one way

MAPS REQUIRED: Dane Canyon Quadrangle; 7.5 minute series topographic, Gila County.

PERMIT: No

WATER: Not dependable

INFORMATION: Summer storms gather very quickly here

ATTRACTION: Almost the easiest way to Highline Trail from Rim Road.

MYRTLE TRAIL

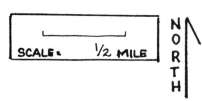

SCALE: ½ MILE

NORTH

LEGEND

- **HARD SURFACE**
- **LIGHT DUTY**
- **UNIMPROVED**
- **TRAIL**
- **RAILROAD**
- **FOOT BRIDGE**
- **BUILDINGS**
- **WATER TANK**
- **CAMPSITE**
- **WINDMILL**
- **x5290 ELEVATION CHECK**
- **MINESHAFT**
- **SPRING**
- **RIM**
- **CORRAL**
- **PEAK**
- **TRAILHEAD**
- **P. PARKING**
- **WATER**
- **RIVER**
- **DRAINAGE**

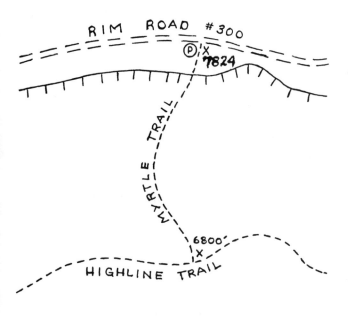

RIM ROAD #300

P X
7824

MYRTLE TRAIL

6800'
X

HIGHLINE TRAIL

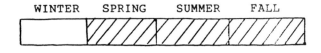

WINTER	SPRING	SUMMER	FALL

DONAHUE TRAIL

Payson Ranger District — (602) 474-2269

DIRECTION: Highline Trail #31 to top of Milk Ranch Point

Donahue Trail is accessible from Highline Trail via Pine Trailhead (1.4 mile) or Redrock Trailhead (3.0 mile). *Entire length of trail is very steep with short switchbacks and lots of loose rock.*

Once trail tops the rim, access to the Rim Road, Turkey Spring Trail, West Webber Trail, and Milk Ranch Point West Trail is available via FR 218 on Milk Ranch Point.

It is quite a challenge to master this trail and one must be prepared for a difficult hike before proceeding. *This is not a trail for a novice hiker.*

REQUIREMENTS: 2 hours hiking time one way; water, food, raingear

LOCATION: 1.5 miles east of Pine trailhead; Tonto National Forest

DIFFICULTY: Moderate to difficult

ELEVATIONS: 5800' to 7200'

LENGTH: 1 mile one way

MAPS REQUIRED: Pine Quadrangle; 7.5 minute series topographic, Gila County.

PERMIT: No

WATER: No

INFORMATION: Extremely hard trail; summer storms gather quickly

ATTRACTION: Quick way to Milk Ranch Point from Pine.

DONAHUE TRAIL

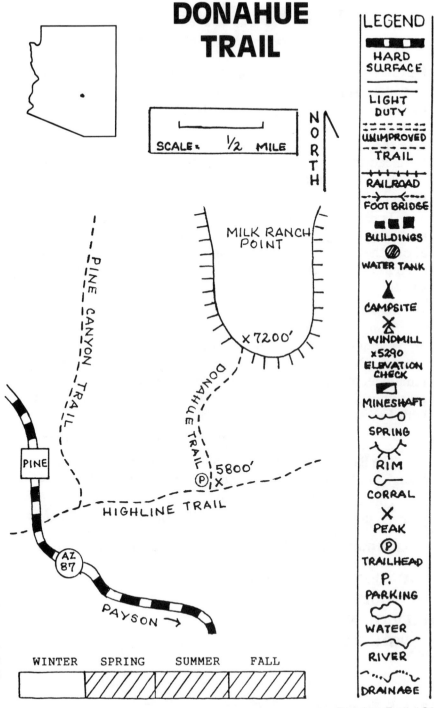

SCALE = ½ MILE

NORTH

MILK RANCH POINT

PINE CANYON TRAIL

DONAHUE TRAIL

×7200'

PINE

Ⓟ 5800'
×

HIGHLINE TRAIL

AZ 87

PAYSON →

WINTER	SPRING	SUMMER	FALL

LEGEND

- ▬ HARD SURFACE
- ── LIGHT DUTY
- ┅ UNIMPROVED TRAIL
- ┼┼┼ RAILROAD
- →)‑‑‑(← FOOT BRIDGE
- ■ ▪ ▪ BUILDINGS
- ⊘ WATER TANK
- ⛺ CAMPSITE
- ✕ WINDMILL
- ×5290 ELEVATION CHECK
- ◣ MINESHAFT
- ∿○ SPRING
- ⌣ RIM
- ⊂ CORRAL
- ✕ PEAK
- Ⓟ TRAILHEAD
- P. PARKING
- ⬯ WATER
- ∿ RIVER
- ⋯ DRAINAGE

BABE HAUGHT TRAIL

Payson Ranger District — (602) 474-2269

DIRECTION: Fish Hatchery up over the rim to Forest Road #300

Take Highway 260 east out of Payson past Control Road to Forest Road #289 and make a left turn here. This road takes you to the parking lot just outside the fish hatchery. You must hike through the fish hatchery property to gain access to the trailhead that is in back of the far buildings. It is best to let people know your plans while on hatchery property. Check for proper signs on a 4X4 post.

Trail starts by left turn out of hatchery area, followed by an abrupt uphill sidehill. Trail has a lot of uphill, getting heavy about the .70 mile mark and continuing to the top. You will encounter a false crest of the rim to be followed by the true crest shortly.

Some areas are rocky but passable and very shady.

You will know when you have reached the true top when you encounter a tree notched with a "T" facing the downhill traveler. Great care must be taken at this point in following the remainder of trail to the trailhead at Forest Road #300. Very few markings are found and only a few cairns. Trail will intersect with Forest Road #300, 27 miles northwest of Highway 260.

(Cairns are piles of stones used as trail markers.)

The Babe Haught Trail was built by Anderson Lee "Babe" Haught and his brother to pack crops and supplies to Winslow.

This area is very primitive which makes it very easy to lose yourself in the remoteness and the fantastic views. It is unique.

REQUIREMENTS: 3 hours hiking time one way; water, food, raingear

LOCATION: Fish Hatchery to Rim Road; Tonto National Forest

DIFFICULTY: Moderate

ELEVATIONS: 6400′ to 7700′

LENGTH: 2.2 miles one way

(continued on page 34)

BABE HAUGHT TRAIL

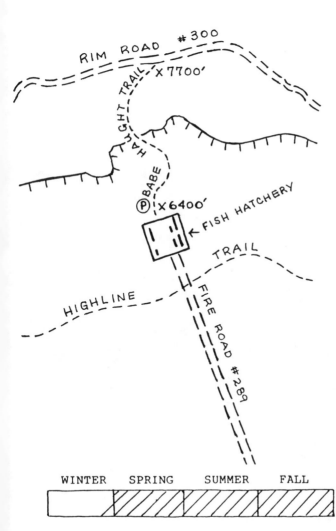

SCALE: 1 MILE

N O R T H

RIM ROAD #300

HAUGHT TRAIL

X 7700'

BABE

ⓟ X 6400'

← FISH HATCHERY

TRAIL

HIGHLINE

FIRE ROAD #289

WINTER	SPRING	SUMMER	FALL

LEGEND

━━━ HARD SURFACE

───── LIGHT DUTY

- - - - UNIMPROVED

- - - TRAIL

+++++ RAILROAD

--->--<--- FOOT BRIDGE

■ ■ ■ BUILDINGS

⊘ WATER TANK

⛺ CAMPSITE

✕ WINDMILL

x5290 ELEVATION CHECK

▱ MINESHAFT

~~o SPRING

⌣⌣⌣ RIM

C CORRAL

✕ PEAK

ⓟ TRAILHEAD

P. PARKING

◯ WATER

~~ RIVER

~··~··~ DRAINAGE

MAPS REQUIRED: Knoll Lake Quadrangle; 7.5 minute series topographic, Gila County.

PERMIT: No

WATER: Not dependable

INFORMATION: Summer storms gather quickly here; historical trail.

ATTRACTION: Fantastic views; remote location.

A pleasing sight from Babe Haught Trail

Looking back from halfway point on Donahue Trail

An inviting area on lower Pine Canyon Trail

PINE CANYON TRAIL

Payson Ranger District — (602) 474-2269

DIRECTION: Rt. #87 south to Pine Trailhead

This is the longest access trail from the north to Pine Trailhead. It is for hikers who love a physical challenge to test their abilities to find their way in some poorly marked areas. *It's no place for a novice to go it alone.*

As it is a very long hike, I would suggest using two cars. This hike can be made in a day, but do start early.

On Rt. 87, continue driving on through Payson until you reach the Pine Trailhead, just south of Pine (well marked). Leaving one car at this location, drive on through Pine on Rt. 87 until mile marker 279.1. Park here and, after you go through the gate, you are at the start of Pine Canyon Trail.

It is imperative that you diligently watch for double-notch markings on the trees to guide you. Concentrate on the markings for the entire length, as many trails branch off along the way. Remember this is Trail No. 26.

At the start of the trail is a fence on the left. *Do not, at any time, cross through it, even though it may seem the way to go. You will come to a gate in the fence at about .2 mile; do not enter, continue straight.*

Soon, stone cairns will appear on the right and the trail gets easier to follow. At .3 mile will be a cairn on the left marking the direct descent, via switchbacks, into Schall Canyon.

Be prepared to take in a fantastic view, as you are about to be enveloped in 100 square miles of nature. So, don't forget your camera.

Even though these switchbacks are in good shape, there will still be a sense of adventure as you descend very quickly. Along with the many pines are alligator junipers, yuccas and sizable manzanita.

At the creek bottom, signs point to places such as "Spradling Canyon", "Cinch Hook Butte", "The Deep Pools" and "Waterfall." They are good reference points, but don't

(continued on page 38)

PINE CANYON TRAIL

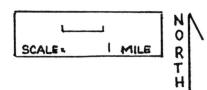

SCALE: |———| 1 MILE

NORTH

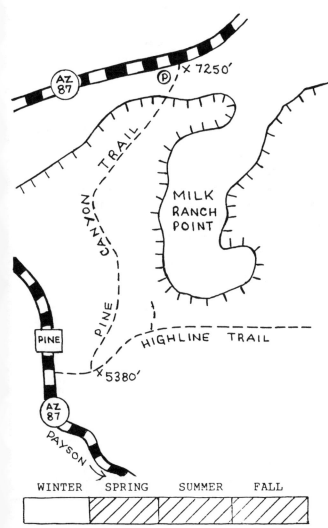

AZ 87

P

× 7250'

PINE CANYON TRAIL

MILK RANCH POINT

HIGHLINE TRAIL

PINE

×5380'

AZ 87

PAYSON →

WINTER	SPRING	SUMMER	FALL

LEGEND

HARD SURFACE

LIGHT DUTY

UNIMPROVED

TRAIL

RAILROAD

FOOT BRIDGE

BUILDINGS

WATER TANK

CAMPSITE

WINDMILL

×5290 ELEVATION CHECK

MINESHAFT

SPRING

RIM

CORRAL

× PEAK

P TRAILHEAD

P. PARKING

WATER

RIVER

DRAINAGE

stray from the trail.

A few miles past the creek is a lovely meadow at "Parsnip Springs."

The spring is flowing about two feet wide along the left side of the trail. The trail here turns into a road, and the black and yellow signs indicate this is a study area.

Watch on the left for a sign that says, "Dripping Springs" and "Highland Trail." *Make a 90° left turn. Continuing straight instead is forbidden, as it is 100% private property.*

After the left turn, the trail will ascend and become more rugged. You will have to become alert now for tree markings. In about a half mile or so, after excellent views of Pine, you will arrive at "Dripping Springs." Here the trail descends very steeply into the drainage, and just as quickly, climbs back out. At the top, the trail forks.

Taking the trail to the right, following white marks and notchings on trees, you will come to an old, small cement tank where pipe is being connected for water. Continue past this and the trail will turn into a graded road.

Follow this road for about one-third of a mile until you arrive at two 10-foot alligator juniper posts on the right, with wires hung between them. Turn left here, and again the trail starts down with a cairn on the right. The trail is very easy from here to Pine Trailhead, which is now very close.

REQUIREMENTS: 6 hours hiking time one way; water, food, sturdy boots, raingear

LOCATION: Northeast of Pine; Tonto National Forest

DIFFICULTY: Moderate

ELEVATIONS: 7250' to 5380'

LENGTH: 7.2 miles one way

MAPS REQUIRED: Pine Quadrangle; 7.5 minute series topographic Gila County.

PERMIT: No

WATER: Not dependable

INFORMATION: Summer storms develop quickly

ATTRACTION: Fantastic views of rim country; huge ponderosa pines.

Alluring scene on Drew Trail

Excellent cover on Horton Creek Trail

HORTON CREEK TRAIL

Payson Ranger District — (602) 474-2269

DIRECTION: Horton Campground north to intersection with Highline Trail #31

Trailhead is in upper corner of campground at intersection of Horton Creek and Forest Road #289. A sign is in place that directs you downhill through a dry wash and up the other side. Hiking now on left side of wash, a cattle gate is encountered at .25 mile. At .70 mile, the trail leaves the wash for a short distance and starts gently uphill. You will find very few markings, but you will almost always be within sound of Horton Creek. Trail follows old logging road most of the time. Area is open and easy hiking.

At 2.70 miles, the trail continues through two 20-foot logs laid on the ground and then turns sharply left. A fork in the trail is encountered at the 3.00 mile mark. Continuing on the right fork along the creek, many small waterfalls are encountered as well as an alligator juniper with a 19-foot circumference. A truly relaxing area here is to be enjoyed.

Shortly after, more rocks are encountered, as well as a few switchbacks. At 3.85 miles, you will intersect with Highline Trail #31 at Horton Spring. This spring always flows generously.

Traveling straight from this intersection will take you to top of the Rim via Horton Spring Trail #292.

A left turn on Highline #31 here takes you to Tonto Creek just below the fish hatchery, and a right turn takes you to Promontory Butte Trail #278, as well as Derrick Trail #33. This is a rewarding hike with many possibilities.

This trail provides good opportunities for short day hikes from Horton Campground, or in combination with lower Derrick makes a good all-day hike.

Unusually large spring at Horton Spring, a popular camping area on Highline Trail. Trout fishing good along

(continued on page 42)

HORTON CREEK TRAIL

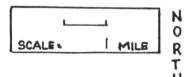

SCALE = 1 MILE

NORTH

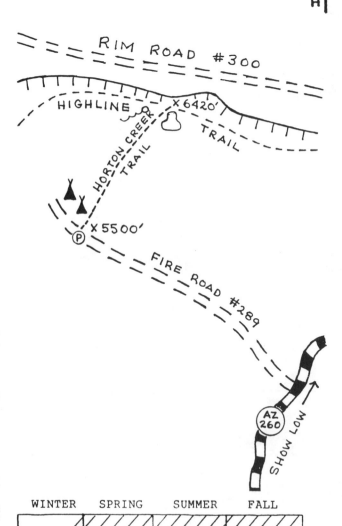

RIM ROAD #300

HIGHLINE TRAIL

x 6420'

HORTON CREEK TRAIL

x 5500'

P

FIRE ROAD #289

AZ 260

SHOW LOW

WINTER	SPRING	SUMMER	FALL

Horton Creek.

Horton Spring Trail #292 from here to top of Rim is very steep. It was used by Zane Grey and Babe Haught to reach hunting area above Rim.

REQUIREMENTS: 2 hours hiking time one way; water, food, raingear

LOCATION: East of Tonto Fish Hatchery; Tonto National Forest

DIFFICULTY: Easy

ELEVATIONS: 5500′ to 6420′

LENGTH: 3.8 miles one way

MAPS REQUIRED: Promontory Butte Quadrangle; 7.5 minute series topographic Gila County.

PERMIT: No

WATER: Available unless weather has been extremely dry.

INFORMATION: Summer storms develop quickly

ATTRACTION: A relaxing hike hearing water flowing for most of the trail

Author snacking with bird on West Fork Trail

Small falls along South Fork Trail

Sign at turnaround point on West Fork Trail

DREW TRAIL

Payson Ranger District — (602) 474-2269

DIRECTION: Descends down off the Rim to its intersection with Highline Trail #31

At a point on Forest Road #300, 5.4 miles northwest of Highway 260, a small gravel road turns left off of Forest Road #300. Take this road a short distance and you will encounter a brown Forest Service sign indicating "Drew Trail."

After passing through a gate here on the left side, the trail descends rapidly but is still easy going. Trail is sometimes very wide and other times narrow and rocky. At 1.10 miles, a right turn onto Highline would take you to Forest Road #284, and a left turn to Highway 260.

Trail is short but makes an excellent way to get to Highline #31 from top of Rim.

Prior to 1909, this trail was blazed from the junction of the Highline at Sharp Creek north over the Rim. It connects with a logging road in the vicinity of Hole-in-the-Ground in the Chevelon Ranger Station.

Road was built to move produce from Winslow by the Drew family that homesteaded around Sharp Creek.

REQUIREMENTS: Half hour hiking time one way; water, snack, raingear

LOCATION: 5.4 miles northwest of AZ Route 260 on Rim Road; Tonto National Forest

DIFFICULTY: Moderate

ELEVATIONS: 7600' to 6750'

LENGTH: 1.1 miles one way

MAPS REQUIRED: Woods Canyon Quadrangle; 7.5 minute series topographic Gila County.

PERMIT: No

WATER: Not dependable

INFORMATION: A little rocky in spots, but a good trail; watch for fast-forming summer storms.

ATTRACTION: Another access to Highline Trail from Rim Road.

DREW TRAIL

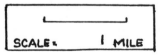

SCALE = 1 MILE

NORTH

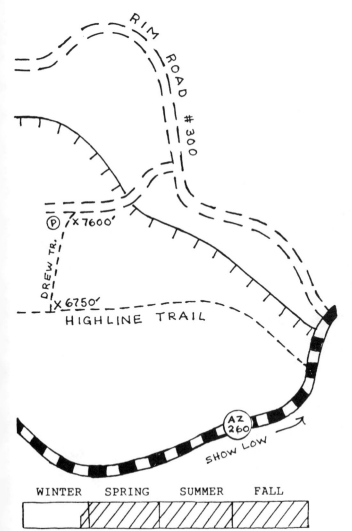

RIM ROAD #300

P ×7600'

DREW TR.

×6750'

HIGHLINE TRAIL

AZ 260

SHOW LOW

WINTER	SPRING	SUMMER	FALL

LEGEND

HARD SURFACE

LIGHT DUTY

UNIMPROVED TRAIL

RAILROAD

FOOT BRIDGE

BUILDINGS

WATER TANK

CAMPSITE

WINDMILL

×5290 **ELEVATION CHECK**

MINESHAFT

SPRING

RIM

CORRAL

PEAK

Ⓟ **TRAILHEAD**

P. **PARKING**

WATER

RIVER

DRAINAGE

EAST WEBBER TRAIL

Payson Ranger District — (602) 474-2269

DIRECTION: Geronimo Boy Scout Camp north to termination

Access to Geronimo Boy Scout Camp is gained by traveling northwest on Route 87 from Payson and making a right turn onto Control Road. Take Control Road to Forest Raod #440 (clearly marked). Turn left here and continue into Geronimo.

Park and then proceed directly to information post and advise them of your intentions.

Access is gained by heading northeast out of Camp Geronimo, past Inspiration Point, which turns into an old sevice road.

East Webber will start ⅛ mile from this point and is marked well with a sign. Trail is marked by blue paint on trees.

This is indeed a fantastic trail as it crosses Webber Creek a total of 7 times, with the entire length being cool and shady. Except for a few large tree falls (36"), the trail is open and easy to follow, and so refreshing.

At its termination at 2.80 miles, directly across the creek is No Name Spring that flows right out of a hole at the base of the Rim. Also here are large flat rocks in the creek to relax on. It is indeed an area you will not want to leave. Return the way you came.

REQUIREMENTS: 1.5 hours hiking time one way; water, snack, raingear

LOCATION: North out of Geronimo Boy Scout Camp; Tonto National Forest

DIFFICULTY: Easy

ELEVATIONS: 5640′ to 6600′

LENGTH: 2.8 miles one way

MAPS REQUIRED: Kehl Ridge Quadrangle; 7.5 minute series topographic Gila County.

PERMIT: No

(continued on page 48)

EAST WEBBER TRAIL

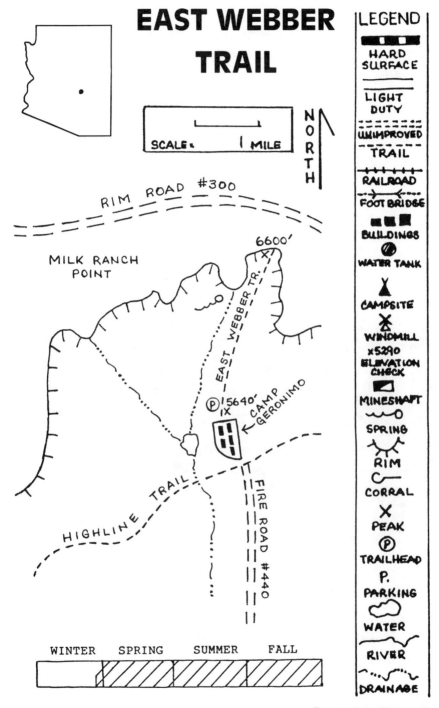

SCALE: 1 MILE

NORTH

LEGEND

HARD SURFACE

LIGHT DUTY

UNIMPROVED TRAIL

RAILROAD

FOOT BRIDGE

BUILDINGS

WATER TANK

CAMPSITE

WINDMILL

x5290 ELEVATION CHECK

MINESHAFT

SPRING

RIM

CORRAL

PEAK

TRAILHEAD

P. PARKING

WATER

RIVER

DRAINAGE

RIM ROAD #300

MILK RANCH POINT

6600'

EAST WEBBER TR.

5640'

CAMP GERONIMO

HIGHLINE TRAIL

FIRE ROAD #440

WINTER   SPRING   SUMMER   FALL

WATER: Available unless weather has been extremely dry.

INFORMATION: Summer storms develop quickly

ATTRACTION: Very nice scenery; listen to the relaxing water flow.

Nearing Rim base on East Webber Trail

Just before entering open area of Derrick Trail

A man-made lean-to on Derrick Spur Trail

DERRICK SPUR TRAIL

Payson Ranger District — (602) 474-2269

DIRECTION: Derrick Trail #33 to Highway 260

Derrick Spur trail starts from Derrick Trail #33 at a point .70 of a mile from Horton Campground.

Trail is indicated at this point by a sign which is visible to the hiker coming downhill on Derrick Trail #33.

This spur trail offers an alternate for travel to Highway 260 instead of the .70 of a mile more which would end at Horton Campground.

Trail traverses a small hill, but travel is easy. It terminates at the intersection of Highway 260 and Forest Road #289.

REQUIREMENTS: Half hour hiking time one way; water, snack, raingear

LOCATION: Northeast of Horton Campground; Tonto National Forest

DIFFICULTY: Easy

ELEVATIONS: 5820' to 5410'

LENGTH: 9/10th mile one way

MAPS REQUIRED: Promontory Butte Quadrangle; 7.5 minute series topographic Gila County.

PERMIT: No

WATER: No

INFORMATION: Watch for fast-forming summer storms

ATTRACTION: Alternate trail to AZ Route 260 from Derrick Trail.

DERRICK SPUR TRAIL

SCALE: 1 MILE

NORTH

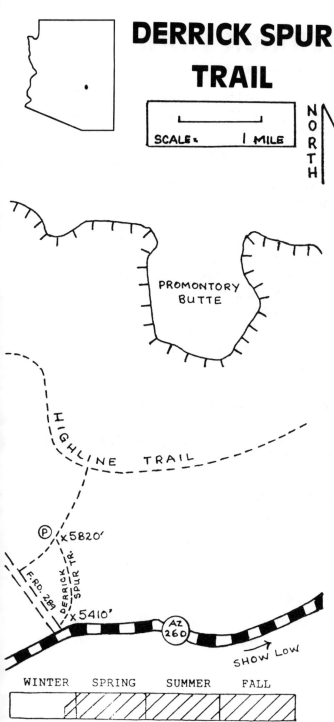

PROMONTORY BUTTE

HIGHLINE TRAIL

P x5820'

F. RD. 289

DERRICK SPUR TR.

x5410'

AZ 260

SHOW LOW

| WINTER | SPRING | SUMMER | FALL |

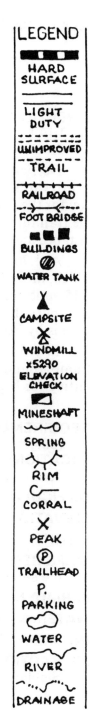

LEGEND

HARD SURFACE

LIGHT DUTY

UNIMPROVED TRAIL

RAILROAD

FOOT BRIDGE

BUILDINGS

WATER TANK

CAMPSITE

WINDMILL

x5290 ELEVATION CHECK

MINESHAFT

SPRING

RIM

CORRAL

PEAK

TRAILHEAD

P. PARKING

WATER

RIVER

DRAINAGE

DERRICK TRAIL

Payson Ranger District — (602) 474-2269

DIRECTION: Start of trail will be at intersection of DERRICK TRAIL #33 and Highline Trail #31 southwest to Horton Creek Campground.

Derrick Trail is well marked at its takeoff from Highline #31 towards the campground. A fence on your left will guide you for the first part of the trail. At about the 1.50 mile mark, the trail turns onto an old service road for only a very short distance and then turns into a trail again.

At 1.70 mile marker is a sign for the "Derrick Spur Trail" which, in .9 of a mile, would take you to Highway 260. At the 2.15 mile marker, the trail makes a sharp left turn as it continues through a gate. Sign here indicates trail maintenance is by Boy Scout Troop #75.

In .15 mile, the trail will terminate at Horton Creek Campground. This trail is clean and open. It is a perfect setting for beginning hikers.

REQUIREMENTS: 3 hours hiking time one way; water, snack, raingear

LOCATION: Northeast out of Horton Creek Campground; Tonto National Forest

DIFFICULTY: Easy

ELEVATIONS: 6610' to 5500'

LENGTH: 2.4 miles one way

MAPS REQUIRED: Promontory Butte Quadrangle; 7.5 minute series topographic Gila County.

PERMIT: No

WATER: Not dependable

INFORMATION: Severe summer storms gather quickly

ATTRACTION: Alternate trail to Horton Campground from Highline Trail.

DERRICK TRAIL

SCALE: |————| 1 MILE

NORTH

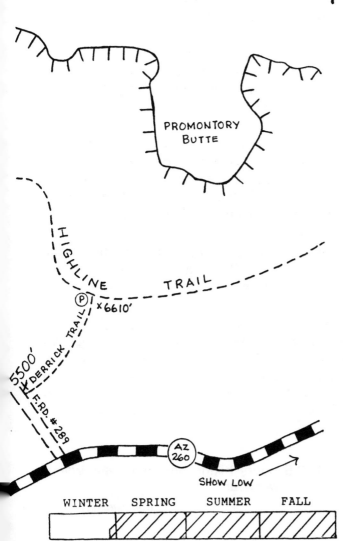

PROMONTORY BUTTE

HIGHLINE TRAIL

(P) ×6610'

5500'
DERRICK TRAIL

F.RD. #289

AZ 260

SHOW LOW

WINTER	SPRING	SUMMER	FALL

LEGEND

HARD SURFACE

LIGHT DUTY

UNIMPROVED TRAIL

RAILROAD

FOOT BRIDGE

BUILDINGS

WATER TANK

CAMPSITE

WINDMILL

×5290 ELEVATION CHECK

MINESHAFT

SPRING

RIM

CORRAL

PEAK

(P) TRAILHEAD

P. PARKING

WATER

RIVER

DRAINAGE

WEST WEBBER TRAIL

Payson Ranger District — (602) 474-2269

DIRECTION: Geronimo Boy Scout Camp up to Milk Ranch Point

Access to Geronimo Boy Scout Camp is gained by traveling northwest on Route 87 from Payson and making a right turn onto Control Road. Take Control Road to Forest Road #440 (clearly marked); turn left here and continue into Geronimo.

Park and then proceed directly to the information post and advise them of your intentions. They will direct you to the trailhead. At .80 mile, you will pass through a gate leaving Geronimo. At 1.00 mile, there will be the sign indicating West Webber Trail.

At 1.10 miles, trail intersects with a road entering from the southwest. Signs with arrows indicate proper path. At 1.55 mile point is a ponderosa pine measuring 12½ feet around —nice point of interest. At 1.70 mile mark you will see your first cairn in a generally rough area, and care must be taken to watch for tree markings.

At the 2.25-mile marker, the trail has a fork; stay on the fork that continues uphill. Trail gets steep with switchbacks. The 2.85 marker is blessed with graffiti instructing you to "have fun."

At the 2.95 marker, you will pass through a gate indicating that you have topped the Rim, although the trail still climbs from this point. You must watch closely from here to follow blaze marks to the Forest Service Road #218 on top of Milk Ranch Point. A left turn on this road would take you to Donahue Trailhead, as a right turn takes you to Turkey Spring Trailhead.

REQUIREMENTS: 2.5 hours hiking time one way; water, snack, sturdy boots, raingear

(continued on page 56)

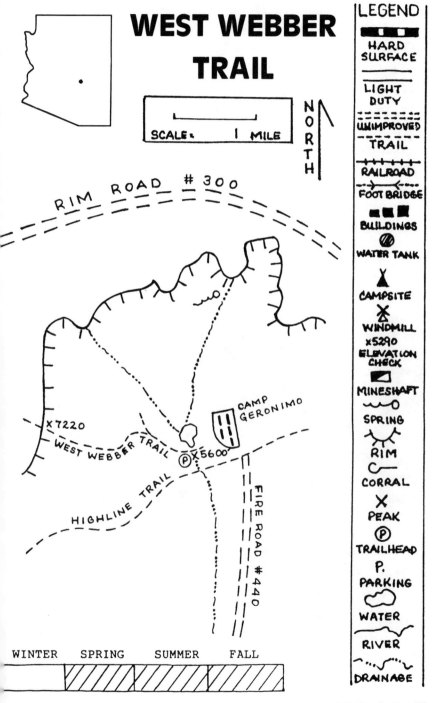

WEST WEBBER TRAIL

SCALE: 1 MILE

NORTH

RIM ROAD # 300

X 7220
WEST WEBBER TRAIL

HIGHLINE TRAIL

CAMP GERONIMO

X 5600
P

FIRE ROAD # 440

WINTER | SPRING | SUMMER | FALL

LEGEND

HARD SURFACE

LIGHT DUTY

UNIMPROVED TRAIL

RAILROAD

FOOT BRIDGE

BUILDINGS

WATER TANK

CAMPSITE

WINDMILL

x5290 ELEVATION CHECK

MINESHAFT

SPRING

RIM

CORRAL

PEAK

TRAILHEAD

P. PARKING

WATER

RIVER

DRAINAGE

West Webber Trail / 55

(West Webber Trail continued)

LOCATION: West of Geronimo Boy Scout Camp to Rim; Tonto National Forest

DIFFICULTY: Difficult

ELEVATIONS: 5600′ to 7220′

LENGTH: 3.15 miles one way

MAPS REQUIRED: Pine Quadrangle; 7.5 minute series topographic Gila County.

PERMIT: No

WATER: No

INFORMATION: Be prepared for this trail; rocky, steep ascent; fast-forming summer storms.

ATTRACTION: Trail is shady and serene

Lush area off West Webber Trail

View descending Col. Devon Trail

Pristine area at Milk Ranch Point — West Trail

MILK RANCH POINT WEST TRAIL

Payson Ranger District — (602) 474-2269

DIRECTION: Alternate trail to Geronimo Scout Camp from Milk Ranch Point

Trailhead is on West Webber Trail descending off the Rim at Milk Ranch Point at the one-mile mark.

If you want to descend back down the West Webber Trail from Milk Ranch Point at the one-mile mark, the Milk Ranch Point West Trail takes off to the right. The trail is in good condition.

At the 2.8-mile marker, the trail intersects with an old road. Make a left turn here. In ¼ mile, it joins the West Webber at Turkey Spring. Turn right here and in ¼ mile, you will be at the Camp Geronimo fence line above sites 5 and 6.

(See West Webber Trail.)

REQUIREMENTS: 1.5 hours hiking time one way; water, snack, raingear, sturdy boots

LOCATION: Off of West Webber Trail; Tonto National Forest

DIFFICULTY: Moderate

ELEVATIONS: 6600′ to 5600′

LENGTH: 2.2 miles one way

MAPS REQUIRED: Pine Quadrangle; 7.5 minute series topographic Gila County.

PERMIT: No

WATER: Not available in dry season

INFORMATION: Summer storms gather quickly

ATTRACTION: Alternate trail back to Camp Geronimo from West Webber Trail.

MILK RANCH POINT WEST TRAIL

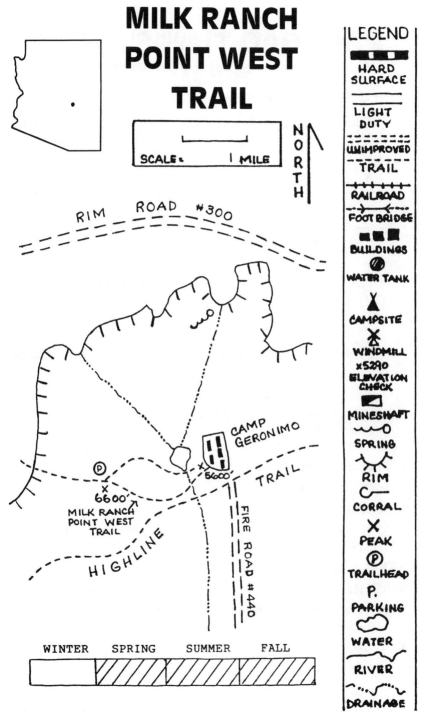

LEGEND

HARD SURFACE

LIGHT DUTY

UNIMPROVED TRAIL

RAILROAD

FOOT BRIDGE

BUILDINGS

WATER TANK

CAMPSITE

WINDMILL

x5290 ELEVATION CHECK

MINESHAFT

SPRING

RIM

CORRAL

PEAK

TRAILHEAD

P. PARKING

WATER

RIVER

DRAINAGE

SCALE: 1 MILE

NORTH

RIM ROAD #300

CAMP GERONIMO

TRAIL

P

X 5600

X 6600

MILK RANCH POINT WEST TRAIL

HIGHLINE

FIRE ROAD #440

WINTER   SPRING   SUMMER   FALL

GILA COUNTY

RAILROAD TUNNEL TRAIL

Payson Ranger District — (602) 474-2269

DIRECTION: Off Col. Devon Trail to tunnel

Trailhead is one mile into Col. Devon Trail. After leaving Forest Road #300, a sign for Railroad Tunnel Trail will appear on your left.

A failed bid to tunnel through the Rim so that trains could pass through, and a stone ruin, can be observed by taking this short side trip (steep). Bear right at all times on this side trip and the tunnel will soon appear.

NOTE:

The Arizona Mineral Belt Railroad in the early 1880's had plans of cashing in on the need for transportation for the precious ore from the Globe area. It required a tunnel through the Rim some 3,100 feet long. After running short of funds twice, it finally was given up and the partial tunnel remains today.

REQUIREMENTS: 1 hour hiking time round trip; water, food, raingear

LOCATION: Off of Col. Devon Trail; Tonto National Forest

DIFFICULTY: Moderate

ELEVATIONS: 6500' to 6800'

LENGTH: .25 mile one way

MAPS REQUIRED: Dane Canyon Quadrangle; 7.5 minute series topographic Gila County.

PERMIT: No

WATER: Available unless weather has been extremely dry.

INFORMATION: Summer storms can be severe and gather quickly

ATTRACTION: Railroad tunnel

RAILROAD TUNNEL TRAIL

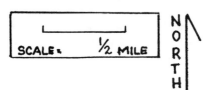

SCALE: ½ MILE

NORTH

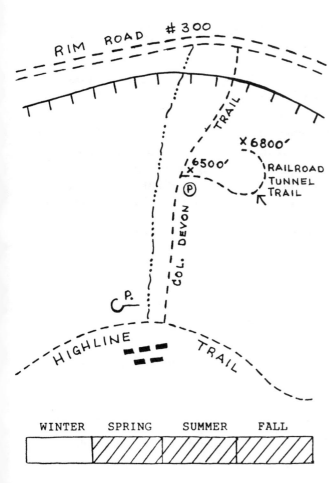

RIM ROAD #300

COL. DEVON TRAIL

×6800'

×6500'

RAILROAD
TUNNEL
TRAIL

P.

P.

HIGHLINE TRAIL

WINTER	SPRING	SUMMER	FALL

LEGEND

HARD SURFACE

LIGHT DUTY

UNIMPROVED

TRAIL

RAILROAD

FOOT BRIDGE

BUILDINGS

WATER TANK

CAMPSITE

WINDMILL

×5290 ELEVATION CHECK

MINESHAFT

SPRING

RIM

CORRAL

PEAK

TRAILHEAD

PARKING

WATER

RIVER

DRAINAGE

COL. DEVON TRAIL

Payson Ranger District — (602) 474-2269

DIRECTION: Trailhead on Forest Road #300 south to Highline Trail at Washington Park

Access to the trailhead is gained by taking Route 87 north through Strawberry until you reach mile marker 281.5. Make a right turn here onto Forest Road #300 and continue east for 12.1 miles.

At this point, there is a sign on your left commemorating the "Apache Battle of Big Dry Wash." Directly across the road is the start of Col. Devon Trail.

Follow this trail bearing left at all times (do not follow power lines), which will put you immediately on a side hill; this is correct. A small sign for downhill travelers indictes a left or right turn. Coming from the top down, a right turn takes you onto the power access trail (wrong); a left turn keeps you on Col. Devon Trail (correct).

A run-down fence now appears on your right side. It is very close to the power line road and actually follows it for a very short distance. It will leave it again at a two-foot cairn via 90° left turn. You will soon find yourself at the upper end of Washington Park and the intersection of Highline Trail.

REQUIREMENTS: 2 hours hiking time one way; water, food, raingear

LOCATION: South of Battle of Big Dry Wash marker; Tonto National Forest

DIFFICULTY: Easy

ELEVATIONS: 7264′ to 6000′

LENGTH: 3.2 miles one way

MAPS REQUIRED: Kehl Ridge Quadrangle; 7.5 minute series topographic Gila County.

PERMIT: No

WATER: Available unless weather has been extremely dry.

INFORMATION: Summer storms gather quickly here.

ATTRACTION: Railroad Tunnel side trip.

COL. DEVON TRAIL

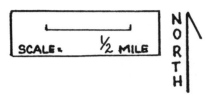

SCALE: ½ MILE

NORTH

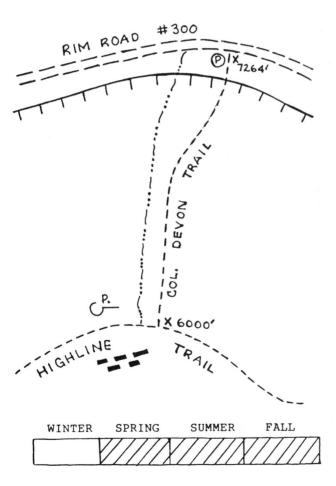

RIM ROAD #300

(P) IX 7264'

COL. DEVON TRAIL

C P.

X 6000'

HIGHLINE TRAIL

WINTER	SPRING	SUMMER	FALL

LEGEND

HARD SURFACE

LIGHT DUTY

UNIMPROVED

TRAIL

RAILROAD

FOOT BRIDGE

BUILDINGS

WATER TANK

CAMPSITE

WINDMILL

x5290 ELEVATION CHECK

MINESHAFT

SPRING

RIM

CORRAL

PEAK

(P) TRAILHEAD

P. PARKING

WATER

RIVER

DRAINAGE

PROMONTORY BUTTE TRAIL

Payson Ranger District — (602) 474-2269

DIRECTION: Highline Trail intersection north to top of Rim on Promontory Butte

Trailhead is located on Highline Trail between Horton Spring Trail and Derrick Trail.

The trail sign, located on Highline Trail, indicates "Promontory Butte ¾ mile." If you undertake this hike and make it to the top, you will have mastered the hardest, most challenging hike that the Rim country has to offer.

This trail, much of the time, is as hard to find as it is rocky and brushy. I cannot really tell you much about the trail except to: take your time, move slowly and study hard before you move.

However, when you do reach the top, you will have a sense of real satisfaction, as the top of the Butte opens into a huge, grassy area with a view that is indescribable. It also offers a perfect view of the parking area at the termination of Highline Trail at State Route 260.

REQUIREMENTS: 1.5 hours hiking time one way; water, food, raingear

LOCATION: North of Christopher Creek Campground; Tonto National Forest

DIFFICULTY: Very, very difficult

ELEVATIONS: 6700' to 7840'

LENGTH: .75 mile one way

MAPS REQUIRED: Promontory Butte Quadrangle; 7.5 minute series topographic Gila County.

PERMIT: No

WATER: No

INFORMATION: Do not take this trail lightly; beware of fast-forming summer storms.

ATTRACTION: Grasslands on top and magnificent veiws from the Rim.

PROMONTORY BUTTE TRAIL

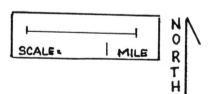

SCALE = I MILE

NORTH

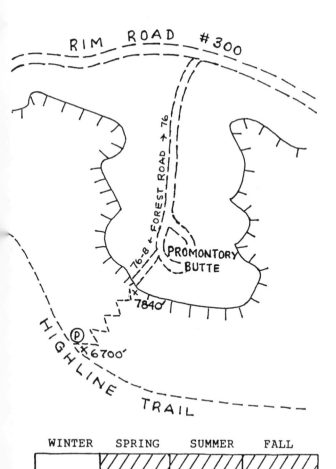

RIM ROAD #300

FOREST ROAD → 76

76-8 ←

PROMONTORY BUTTE

x 7840'

P x 6700'

HIGHLINE TRAIL

| WINTER | SPRING | SUMMER | FALL |

LEGEND

HARD SURFACE

LIGHT DUTY

UNIMPROVED TRAIL

RAILROAD

FOOT BRIDGE

BUILDINGS

WATER TANK

CAMPSITE

WINDMILL

x5290 ELEVATION CHECK

MINESHAFT

SPRING

RIM

CORRAL

PEAK

TRAILHEAD

P. PARKING

WATER

RIVER

DRAINAGE

PARKER CREEK TRAIL

Pleasant Valley Ranger District — (602) 462-3311

DIRECTION: Experimental Station to intersection with Rim Trail

Take Route 60 east to Route 88 just outside Claypool and turn left. Take Route 88 to Route 288 (Young Road), turn right and continue for 29 miles, ten of which are not paved but in good condition.

When you arrive at the sign indicating Sierra Ancha Experimental Forest, continue for about 300 feet where a small road goes to the right leading to the station. A short distance up the road, it will be blocked to vehicles, but there is ample room to park.

Continue walking up the road, past the gate, and turn right at the first T in the road. Then 150 feet further, you will be at the trailhead.

The trail is in excellent condition and ample in width, with many switchbacks to help you on your way. *But one must take care on this trail — it is a long roll to the bottom in many places.*

Although this trail does not go to Aztec Peak, your stopping point on a high, flat plateau leaves you only 614 feet short of its summit, as far as altitude is concerned. However, you're still a good quarter-mile away.

Along the way, you will encounter four types of vegetation, three rocky slopes, numerous pinnacle and geological formations, including spectacular views of Roosevelt Lake and the Four Peaks Wilderness area. This trail terminates at the junction with Rim Trail #139.

REQUIREMENTS: 3-4 hours hiking time round trip; food, water, raingear

LOCATION: Sierra Ancha Experimental Forest

DIFFICULTY: Moderate

ELEVATIONS: 5080' to 7080'

(continued on page 68)

PARKER CREEK TRAIL

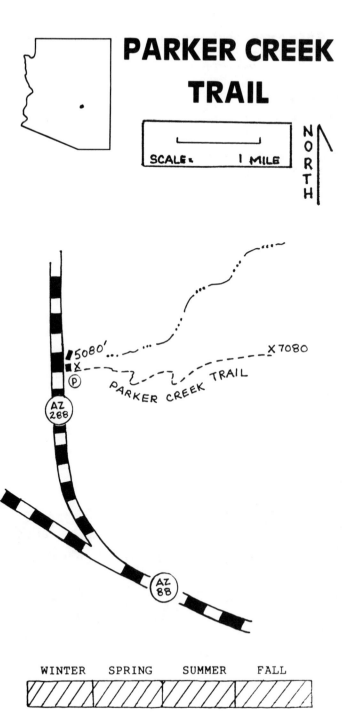

SCALE = 1 MILE

NORTH

5080'
X
Ⓟ
PARKER CREEK TRAIL
X 7080

AZ 288

AZ 88

WINTER	SPRING	SUMMER	FALL

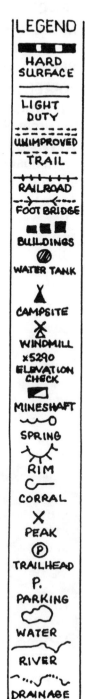

LEGEND

HARD SURFACE

LIGHT DUTY

UNIMPROVED TRAIL

RAILROAD

FOOT BRIDGE

BUILDINGS

WATER TANK

CAMPSITE

WINDMILL

x5290 ELEVATION CHECK

MINESHAFT

SPRING

RIM

CORRAL

X PEAK

Ⓟ TRAILHEAD

P. PARKING

WATER

RIVER

DRAINAGE

(Parker Creek Trail continued)

LENGTH: 3 miles one way

MAPS REQUIRED: Aztec Peak Quadrangle; 7.5 minute series topographic Gila County.

PERMIT: No

WATER: Not guaranteed

INFORMATION: Be sure to pace yourself; look for insulators from old telegraph lines.

ATTRACTION: Four vegetation types to hike through — unusual geological features.

Promontory Butte viewed from Highline Trail

On Parker Creek Trail

Redrock Spring tank on Redrock Trail

REDROCK TRAIL

Payson Ranger District — (602) 474-2269

DIRECTION: Control Road north to Highline #31

From intersection of SR 87 and Control Road, proceed east on Control Road approximately 2.4 miles to trailhead.

First half mile of trail follows old jeep road. Trail then leaves old road and proceeds uphill to the base of the Rim and an intersection with the Highline Trail #31.

Redrock Spring is approximately 100 yards to the left of the actual intersection of the two trails and is a reliable water stop.

A left-hand turn at Highline #31 gives access to Donahue Trail #27, Pine Canyon Trail #26 and, eventually, the Pine Trailhead itself.

A right turn on Highline #31 takes you to Camp Geronimo and beyond.

Redrock Trail #294 is a perfect access trail for Highline #31.

REQUIREMENTS: Half hour hiking time one way; water, snack, raingear

LOCATION: Control Road 2.5 miles east of AZ Route 87; Tonto National Forest

DIFFICULTY: Easy

ELEVATIONS: 5600′ to 6000′

LENGTH: 1 mile one way

MAPS REQUIRED: Buckhead Mesa Quadrangle; 7.5 minute series topographic Gila County.

PERMIT: No

WATER: At Redrock Spring

INFORMATION: Summer storms gather quickly here

ATTRACTION: Perfect access to Highline Trail from Control Road.

REDROCK TRAIL

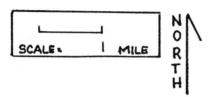

SCALE = 1 MILE

NORTH

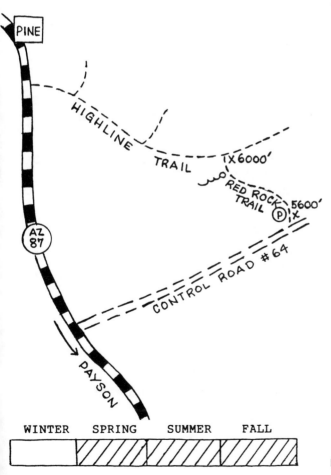

PINE

HIGHLINE TRAIL

X 6000'

RED ROCK TRAIL

Ⓟ 5600'
X

AZ 87

CONTROL ROAD #64

PAYSON

WINTER	SPRING	SUMMER	FALL

LEGEND

HARD SURFACE

LIGHT DUTY

UNIMPROVED

TRAIL

RAILROAD

FOOT BRIDGE

BUILDINGS

WATER TANK

CAMPSITE

WINDMILL

x5290
ELEVATION CHECK

MINESHAFT

SPRING

RIM

CORRAL

PEAK

Ⓟ TRAILHEAD

P.
PARKING

WATER

RIVER

DRAINAGE

HORTON SPRING TRAIL

Payson Ranger District — (602) 474-2269

DIRECTION: From Forest Road #300 southwest to Highline #31.

Access to this trailhead is from a point on Forest Road #300, 24 miles from Highway 260.

Trail is well-marked at the top, indicating Horton Spring Trail #292. *The entire first half of this trail is a sidehill, very steep, rocky and with switchbacks as well. Care must be taken until you are past this point not to fall or twist an ankle.* This is indeed a very primitive area and not well-traveled at all.

At 1.10 miles, the trail starts to widen very nicely. At 1.25 miles is Horton Spring itself, understandably a very popular camping spot.

At 1.35 miles is the intersection with Highline Trail #31. Eastbound travel from here takes you to Promontory Trail as well as Derrick Trail. Westbound travel takes you to the Fish Hatchery. *Horton Spring Trail is not for a novice hiker.*

REQUIREMENTS: 1.5 hours hiking time one way; water, food, raingear, sturdy boots

LOCATION: 24 miles northwest of AZ 260 on Fire Road #300

DIFFICULTY: Difficult

ELEVATIONS: 7800′ to 6420′

LENGTH: 1.35 miles one way

MAPS REQUIRED: Promontory Butte Quadrangle; 7.5 minute series topographic Gila County.

PERMIT: No

WATER: At Horton Spring

INFORMATION: Be very careful on this trail; side hill, loose rock; fast-forming summer storms.

ATTRACTION: Scenic area around Horton Spring.

HORTON SPRING
TRAIL

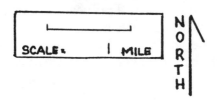

SCALE = 1 MILE

NORTH

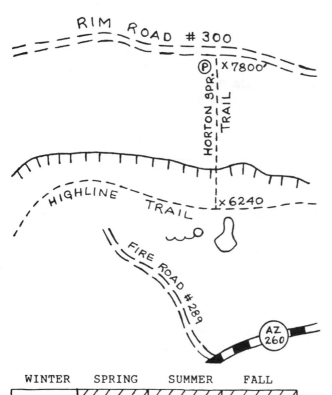

RIM ROAD # 300

Ⓟ ╎ X 7800

HORTON SPR. TRAIL

x 6240

HIGHLINE TRAIL

FIRE ROAD # 289

AZ 260

WINTER	SPRING	SUMMER	FALL

BARNHARDT TRAIL

Payson Ranger District — (602) 474-2269

DIRECTION: Barnhardt Trailhead to Divide Trail

To reach Barnhardt Trailhead, take State Highway 87 toward Payson for 62 miles north of Mesa. A sign indicates a left turn to the trailhead. After turning, a five-mile gravel road, suitable for passenger cars, will lead you to the trailhead.

The trail starts out wide and rocky but gets more distinct as you proceed. After .4 mile, you will pass through a wilderness boundary sign and, at 1.4 miles, you will already have climbed 420 feet. You will next encounter a series of switchbacks high on the left side of a drainage.

At this point, the trail angles to the right, and at the second tributary, just over three miles from the start, there is a narrow canyon that, during heavy snow melt or the monsoon season, contains a cascading waterfall of at least 50 feet.

Continuing now, as you skirt a very deep canyon to say the least, you will next encounter a trail called Sandy Saddle Trail that branches to the right, but continue straight ahead. I was a little amazed to find the mixture of ponderosa pine and manzanita up so high as you near the end of the trail at Divide Trail.

A left turn here would allow you to intersect with Shaketree Trail and return to Barnhardt trailhead at the parking lot.

REQUIREMENTS: 3.5 hours hiking time one way; water, food, raingear

LOCATION: Barnhardt Canyon; Mazatzal Wilderness.

DIFFICULTY: Moderate to difficult

ELEVATIONS: 4200′ to 5650′

LENGTH: 6 miles one way

MAPS REQUIRED: Mazatzal Peak Quadrangle; 7.5 minute series topographic Maricopa County.

(continued on page 76)

BARNHARDT
TRAIL

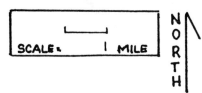

SCALE: |___| MILE

NORTH

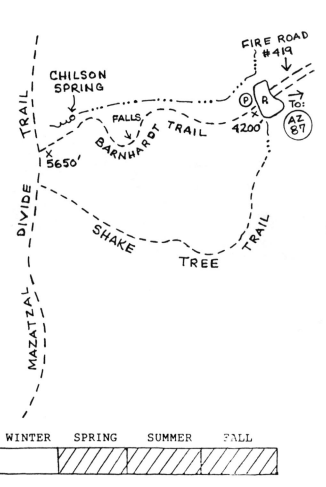

CHILSON SPRING

DIVIDE TRAIL

FALLS

BARNHARDT TRAIL

x 5650'

SHAKE TREE TRAIL

MAZATZAL

FIRE ROAD #419

P R

x 4200'

To: AZ 87

| WINTER | SPRING | SUMMER | FALL |

LEGEND

HARD SURFACE

LIGHT DUTY

UNIMPROVED TRAIL

RAILROAD

FOOT BRIDGE

BUILDINGS

WATER TANK

CAMPSITE

WINDMILL

x5290 ELEVATION CHECK

MINESHAFT

SPRING

RIM

CORRAL

PEAK

TRAILHEAD

P. PARKING

WATER

RIVER

DRAINAGE

PERMIT: No

WATER: Not dependable

INFORMATION: Summer storms gather quickly

ATTRACTION: Excellent trail to Mazatzal Divide Trail — waterfall in season.

Starting down before it gets rocky on Horton Spring Trail

On Hieroglyphic Trail

Ancient writing on Hieroglyphic Trail

HIEROGLYPHIC TRAIL

Mesa Ranger District — (602) 835-1161

DIRECTION: Trailhead to Hieroglyphics

To get to Hieroglyphic Canyon, travel east on Route 60 east of Apache Junction to Kings Ranch Road and take the following route: north on Kings Ranch Road 2.8 miles to Baseline and turn right; .3 mile to Mohican and turn left; .4 mile to Valley View and turn left again; Valley View will turn into N. Whitetail.

Go .5 mile to a T and turn right onto East Cloudview, then proceed the last .3 mile to the parking lot. There is no sign for the trail, but it is evident where it starts at the east end of the lot. The last .3 mile of road is rocky but can be driven by car if you take your time.

This is a spacious trail, and the altitude gain is very gentle. Most of the trail is on top of a ridge (my favorite kind of trail), affording excellent views in all directions.

Slowly but surely, the canyon walls close in on you and some small pools of water will appear just as the trail simply ends. Look to your left and the carvings will be visible.

REQUIREMENTS: 2 hours hiking time one way; water, snack,

LOCATION: Kings Ranch; Superstition Mountains

DIFFICULTY: Easy

ELEVATIONS: 2050′ to 2675′

LENGTH: 3.5 miles round trip

MAPS REQUIRED: Weaver's Needle Quadrangle; 7.5 minute series topographic Maricopa County.

PERMIT: No

WATER: Not during dry time of year.

INFORMATION: Extremely dry and hot in summer months.

ATTRACTION: Numerous hieroglyphs.

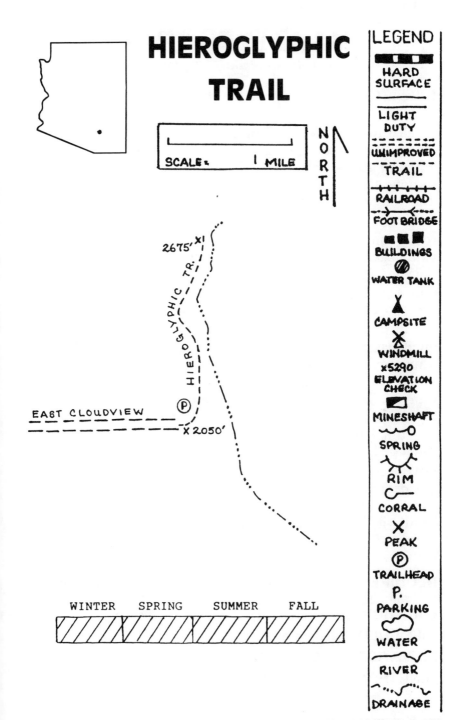

HIEROGLYPHIC TRAIL

SCALE = 1 MILE

NORTH

2675' X'

HIEROGLYPHIC TR.

EAST CLOUDVIEW

P

X 2050'

WINTER | SPRING | SUMMER | FALL

LEGEND

HARD SURFACE

LIGHT DUTY

UNIMPROVED TRAIL

RAILROAD

FOOT BRIDGE

BUILDINGS

WATER TANK

CAMPSITE

WINDMILL

x5290 ELEVATION CHECK

MINESHAFT

SPRING

RIM

CORRAL

PEAK

TRAILHEAD

P. PARKING

WATER

RIVER

DRAINAGE

SHAKETREE TRAIL

Payson Ranger District — (602) 474-2269

DIRECTION: Trailhead from Barnhardt parking lot to Divide Trail

To reach Shaketree Trailhead, take State Highway 87 toward Payson for 62 miles north of Mesa. A sign indicates a left turn to the Barnhardt Trailhead parking area. After turning, a five-mile gravel road suitable for passenger cars will lead you to the trailhead.

The trail heads south, marked with cairns. The trail is rocky and always uphill, but gentle for the most part. A few switchbacks are encountered as you near the path across Suicide Ridge. The trail winds its way around five drainages in only a short distance. It gets quite rocky as you are afforded views of Cactus Ridge with all its unique formations.

Just after the fifth drainage, the trail goes sharply left and uphill past a ridge. Resuming, you traverse to the north side of a huge ravine. It is now very rocky and narrow in places. At 4.5 miles, you reach a sandy saddle at the head of Shaketree Canyon. This makes for an excellent rest stop (even a nap) before descending rapidly into Y-BAR Basin.

When leaving the basin, you will again travel uphill and come to a very faint junction in the trail (approximately 300 feet). Here you must travel to the right and continue to the Divide Trail. From the Divide Trail can be seen Mazatzals west face of almost 1,000-foot cliffs. A right turn on Divide Trail will intersect with Barnhardt Trail and back to the Barnhardt parking area.

REQUIREMENTS: 5 hours hiking time one way; water, food, raingear

LOCATION: Shaketree Canyon; Mazatzal Wilderness

DIFFICULTY: Moderate

ELEVATIONS: 4200' to 6040'

LENGTH: 7.5 miles one way

(continued on page 82)

SHAKETREE TRAIL

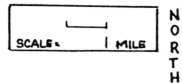

SCALE = 1 MILE

NORTH

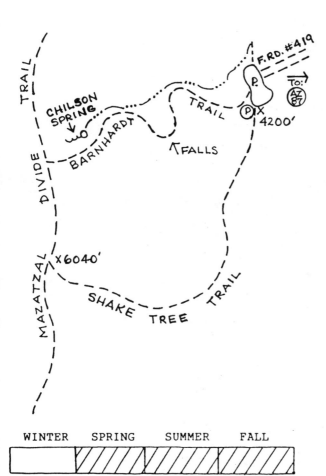

TRAIL

CHILSON SPRING

BARNHARDT

FALLS

F.RD. #419

P.

P X 4200'

To: AZ 87

DIVIDE

MAZATZAL

x6040'

SHAKE TREE TRAIL

WINTER   SPRING   SUMMER   FALL

LEGEND

HARD SURFACE

LIGHT DUTY

UNIMPROVED

TRAIL

RAILROAD

FOOT BRIDGE

BUILDINGS

WATER TANK

CAMPSITE

WINDMILL

x5290 ELEVATION CHECK

MINESHAFT

SPRING

RIM

CORRAL

PEAK

TRAILHEAD

P. PARKING

WATER

RIVER

DRAINAGE

MAPS REQUIRED: Mazatzal Quadrangle; 7.5 minute series topographic Maricopa County.

PERMIT: No

WATER: Not dependable

INFORMATION: Summer storms gather quickly here. Scorching hot in summer.

ATTRACTION: Excellent trail to use with others to skirt Mazatzal Peak

Rock features carved by wind and water on Shaketree Trail

View of rock formation on Echo Canyon Trail

Through small tunnel on Hidden Valley Trail

HIDDEN VALLEY TRAIL

City of Phoenix Parks & Recreation Dept. — (602) 262-4986

DIRECTION: Upper Trailhead off Summit Road to intersection with National Trail

To get to South Mountain Park, take Central Avenue until it dead ends south of Phoenix. To get to Hidden Valley, the tunnel and Natural Bridge, take Summit Road for 1.5 miles into the park to a fork in the road. Continue on the left fork for 3.2 miles to a second fork. Take the right branch for seven-tenths of a mile to yet another fork leading to the television towers. Continue to the left for four-tenths of a mile to the parking area and trailhead. A sign indicates 1¾ miles to Hidden Valley.

After hiking through this rocky, dry terrain for about a mile, you will start dropping into a little canyon on your left. Hike the right side of this canyon.

Soon you will come to a junction in the trail with a sign indicating a right-hand turn for Hidden Valley-Fat Man Pass. The reason it is called Hidden Valley is because it seems as though the trail ends at this point.

As you slide down over a few large rocks, it gets very interesting, geologically, as many cracks and crannies beg to be explored. Two areas exist where you slide down over rocks and they are almost as slick as ice.

Soon you will encounter the tunnel, which is 4 feet wide and 50 feet long. You will want to spend time exploring this feature as well as resting before heading back.

REQUIREMENTS: 3.5 hours hiking time round trip; water, snack, good hiking boots
LOCATION: South Mountain Park, Phoenix
DIFFICULTY: Moderate
ELEVATIONS: 2200' to 2000'
LENGTH: 2 miles one way

(continued on page 86)

HIDDEN VALLEY TRAIL

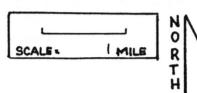

SCALE = 1 MILE

NORTH

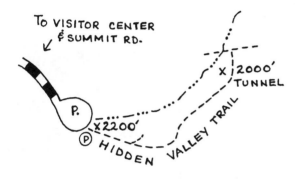

To VISITOR CENTER & SUMMIT RD.

P.

X 2200

HIDDEN VALLEY TRAIL

X 2000' TUNNEL

WINTER	SPRING	SUMMER	FALL

LEGEND

HARD SURFACE

LIGHT DUTY

UNIMPROVED TRAIL

RAILROAD

FOOT BRIDGE

BUILDINGS

WATER TANK

CAMPSITE

WINDMILL

x5290 ELEVATION CHECK

MINESHAFT

SPRING

RIM

CORRAL

PEAK

TRAILHEAD

P. PARKING

WATER

RIVER

DRAINAGE

MAPS REQUIRED: Lone Butte Quadrangle; 7.5 minute series topographic Maricopa County.

PERMIT: No

WATER: No

INFORMATION: Fee is charged entering the park; trail is flood path during rainy weather.

ATTRACTION: Natural tunnel — fine vistas.

Looking at Sugarloaf Mountain from Sugarloaf Trail

En route to bridge on Natural Bridge Trail

Weaver's Needle from Fremont Saddle on Peralta Trail

PERALTA TRAIL

Mesa Ranger District — (602) 835-1161

DIRECTION: Peralta Trailhead to Fremont Saddle at Weaver's needle

To get to the trailhead, take Route #60 eight miles east of Apache Junction, then turn left onto Peralta Road and travel 7.3 miles. This is a dirt road but well-maintained and suitable for passenger cars.

After you have passed the Don's Camp on your left, you will soon come to a large parking area and trailhead.

As you start your hike, the canyon walls not only rise on both sides, but close in on you as well. You will come to shady spots to rest. You will be amazed at all the evidence of erosion that took place on the canyon walls.

At this point, you will be within ten minutes of Fremont Saddle, and there Weaver's Needle will suddenly appear.

REQUIREMENTS: 3-4 hours hiking time round trip; water, snack, raingear

LOCATION: Superstition Mountains; 15 miles northeast of Apache Junction.

DIFFICULTY: Moderate

ELEVATIONS: 2400' to 3800'

LENGTH: 2 miles one way

MAPS REQUIRED: Weaver's Needle Quadrangle; 7.5 minute series topographic Maricopa County.

PERMIT: No

WATER: Not dependable at all

INFORMATION: Canyon prone to treacherous flash flooding and severe storms during rainy periods.

ATTRACTION: Weaver's Needle — legendary home of the Lost Dutchman's gold.

PERALTA TRAIL

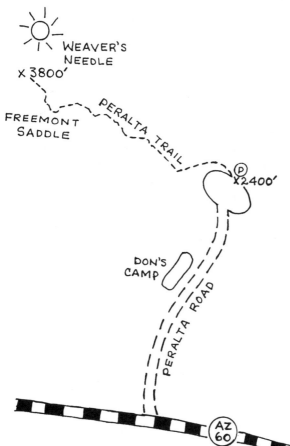

SCALE = 1 MILE

NORTH

WEAVER'S NEEDLE
x 3800'

FREEMONT SADDLE

PERALTA TRAIL

x 2400'

DON'S CAMP

PERALTA ROAD

AZ 60

WINTER	SPRING	SUMMER	FALL

LEGEND

HARD SURFACE

LIGHT DUTY

UNIMPROVED

TRAIL

RAILROAD

FOOT BRIDGE

BUILDINGS

WATER TANK

CAMPSITE

WINDMILL

x5290 ELEVATION CHECK

MINESHAFT

SPRING

RIM

CORRAL

PEAK

TRAILHEAD

P. PARKING

WATER

RIVER

DRAINAGE

FOUR PEAKS TRAIL

Mesa Ranger District — (602) 835-1161

DIRECTION: Trailhead to sign indicating private property on trail skirting peaks.

Access to trailhead is gained by taking State Highway 87 toward Payson. About 21 miles from Mesa, a small sign on the right indicates Four Peaks Road. A truck is recommended, as the road turns to dirt for the next 22 miles.

At about the 19-mile mark, the road will T; traveling to the right here will take you to the parking area in about two more miles. The trail starts at the fence on the right side of the parking lot.

I have made this climb six times and was rained and hailed on five of them. *The trail is very steep in places and only a veteran hiker should attempt this climb.*

After crossing the fence many times and what seems like endless, unforgiving trail, you will arrive at a saddle just before the top. At this point, you will have traveled 7,400 feet from the parking lot, with an elevation gain of 1,150 feet.

Only a couple of hundred feet further, a small trail takes off to the right (very faint) and skirts the peaks for just under two more miles. Use your topographical map here; know how to read it.

You will soon come to a sign indicating private property. Do observe this sign and make this your turn-around point. *This is not a trail for a novice.*

REQUIREMENTS: 6-7 hours hiking time round trip; water, food, good hiking boots, raingear

LOCATION: 24 miles northeast of Mesa in Mazatzal Mountains.

DIFFICULTY: Very difficult

ELEVATIONS: 5700' to 7050'

LENGTH: 3.5 miles one way

MAPS REQUIRED: Four Peaks Quadrangle; 7.5 minute series topographic Maricopa County.

(continued on page 92)

FOUR PEAKS
TRAIL

SCALE = 1 MILE

NORTH

LEGEND

HARD SURFACE

LIGHT DUTY

UNIMPROVED

TRAIL

RAILROAD

FOOT BRIDGE

BUILDINGS

WATER TANK

CAMPSITE

WINDMILL

x5290 ELEVATION CHECK

MINESHAFT

SPRING

RIM

CORRAL

PEAK

℗ TRAILHEAD

P. PARKING

WATER

RIVER

DRAINAGE

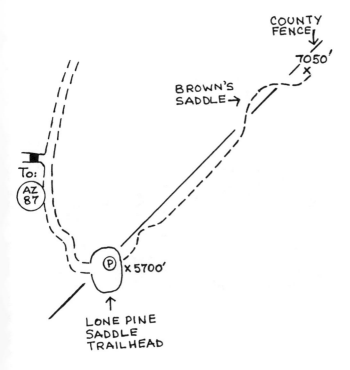

COUNTY FENCE

7050'
X

BROWN'S SADDLE →

To: AZ 87

℗ X 5700'

↑
LONE PINE SADDLE TRAILHEAD

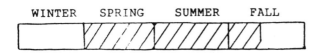

WINTER   SPRING   SUMMER   FALL

PERMIT: No

WATER: No

INFORMATION: Storms are numerous; steep ascent. ***Do not attempt unless you're in very good physical condition.***

ATTRACTION: Magnificent views.

Misty morning view on Four Peaks Trail

Bonita Trail just before entering Mica Meadow

Looking down 80 feet from Waterfall Trail

WATERFALL TRAIL

Maricopa County Parks & Recreation Dept. — (602) 272-8871

DIRECTION: Trailhead to Falls

White Tank Mountain Regional Park is 15 miles west of Glendale on Olive/Dunlap Avenue. You will enter the park on White Tank Mountain Road. Follow this road for several miles and make a left turn onto Waterfall Canyon Road. The trailhead is ¼ mile futher on Waterfall Canyon Road and is marked and signed.

On this short trail, at the half-way mark, are petroglyphs (900-1300 AD). You would do well to keep an eye peeled for petroglyphs the rest of the way.

If you are careful to hike this fascinating trail during a rainy spell, or in the winter, at the end you will be treated to many petroglyphs and an 80-foot waterfall as well. A true oasis in our desert.

REQUIREMENTS: 2 hours hiking time round trip; water, snack

LOCATION: Western Maricopa County; White Tank Mountain Park.

DIFFICULTY: Easy

ELEVATIONS: 1560' to 2480'

LENGTH: 1.5 miles one way

MAPS REQUIRED: White Mountain Quadrangle, Southeast; 7.5 minute series topographic Maricopa County.

PERMIT: No

WATER: Not in dry season

INFORMATION: Very hot in summer weather

ATTRACTION: Petroglyphs and an 80-foot waterfall.

WATERFALL TRAIL

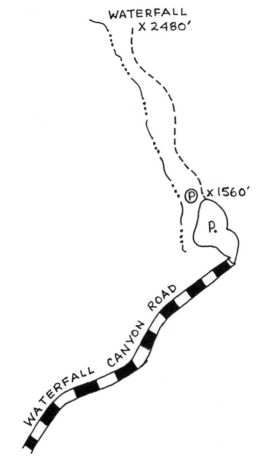

SCALE = 1 MILE

NORTH

WATERFALL X 2480'

X 1560'

P.

WATERFALL CANYON ROAD

WINTER	SPRING	SUMMER	FALL

BONITA TRAIL

Saguaro National Monument East — (602) 296-8576

DIRECTION: Fire Loop Trail to intersection with Mica Meadow Trail

Trailhead is found by leaving Mica Mountain Peak and traveling northeast on Fire Loop Trail for .1 mile to intersection with Mica Mountain Trail, continuing straight on Fire Loop Trail for .1 mile more where Bonita Trail heads south.

Hiking is easy, as the trail makes its way down through the magnificent canopy up above. It is open down below with no clutter of any kind, and the trail is wide.

The canopy slowly begins to open as you make your way to Mica Meadow. Soon there is no canopy; it is now open, with a very obvious trail now making its way through a seemingly endless field of ferns to its intersection with Mica Meadow Trail.

REQUIREMENTS: Half hour hiking time one way; water, food, raingear

LOCATION: East end of Rincon Mountains; Saguaro National Monument East

DIFFICULTY: Easy

ELEVATIONS: 8360' to 8280'

LENGTH: .8 mile one way

MAPS REQUIRED: Mica Mountain Quadrangle; 7.5 minute series topographic Pima County.

PERMIT: No — unless camping overnight; permit available Saguaro National Monument East

WATER: No

INFORMATION: Storms gather quickly here

ATTRACTION: Attractive open grassy areas; alternate way back to Manning Camp.

BONITA TRAIL

SCALE = 1 MILE

NORTH

LEGEND

- **HARD SURFACE**
- **LIGHT DUTY**
- **UNIMPROVED TRAIL**
- **RAILROAD**
- **FOOT BRIDGE**
- **BUILDINGS**
- **WATER TANK**
- **CAMPSITE**
- **WINDMILL**
- x5290 **ELEVATION CHECK**
- **MINESHAFT**
- **SPRING**
- **RIM**
- **CORRAL**
- **PEAK**
- **TRAILHEAD**
- P. **PARKING**
- **WATER**
- **RIVER**
- **DRAINAGE**

FIRE LOOP TRAIL

X MICA MTN. PEAK

(P) X 8360

MICA MOUNTAIN TRAIL

BONITA TRAIL

X 8280'

MICA MEADOW TRAIL

MICA

To MANNING CAMP

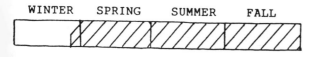

WINTER   SPRING   SUMMER   FALL

MICA MEADOW TRAIL

Saguaro National Monument East — (602) 296-8576

DIRECTION: Lower end of Bonita Trail to intersection with Mica Mountain Trail

Trailhead is at the lower terminus of Bonita Trail.

As it was at the lower end of Bonita Trail, with the lush open area of ferns, Mica Meadow Trail now starts out through the same kind of area and also is gently downhill.

In about .2 mile, almost at the same time the ferns give way to forest, Fire Loop Trail continues to the south. Continue straight for .6 mile as the trail slowly winds its way to Mica Mountain Trail where it ends.

A left turn here takes you to Manning Camp in .5 mile.

REQUIREMENTS: Half hour hiking time one way; water, food, raingear

LOCATION: East end of Rincon Mountains; Saguaro National Monument East.

DIFFICULTY: Easy

ELEVATIONS: 8280' to 8100'

LENGTH: .8 mile one way

MAPS REQUIRED: Mica Mountain Quadrangle; 7.5 minute series topographic Pima County.

PERMIT: No, unless camping overnight; permit available at Saguaro National Monumnt East.

WATER: No

INFORMATION: Storms gather quickly here.

ATTRACTION: Alternate trail back to Manning Camp.

MICA MEADOW
TRAIL

SCALE=   1 MILE

NORTH

FIRE LOOP TRAIL

MICA MTN. PEAK ×

MICA MOUNTAIN TRAIL

BONITA TRAIL

Ⓟ

× 8280'

TRAIL

× 8100'

MICA MEADOW

To MANNING CAMP

WINTER   SPRING   SUMMER   FALL

LEGEND

HARD SURFACE

LIGHT DUTY

UNIMPROVED

TRAIL

RAILROAD

FOOT BRIDGE

BUILDINGS

WATER TANK

CAMPSITE

WINDMILL

×5290 ELEVATION CHECK

MINESHAFT

SPRING

RIM

CORRAL

PEAK

Ⓟ TRAILHEAD

P. PARKING

WATER

RIVER

DRAINAGE

DEVIL'S BATHTUB TRAIL

Saguaro National Monument East — (602) 296-8576

DIRECTION: Heartbreak Ridge to Manning Camp Trail

The trail starts at an area on Heartbreak Ridge Trail called Four Corners and is well marked as Devil's Bathtub Trail.

Devil's Bathtub Trail is 1.2 miles long with only minor ups and downs. You are in for a treat on this trail because, in only .6 mile, you arrive at the bathtub itself at the top of the falls. It is here the water starts its 50-foot fall to the bathtub below.

The waterfall, as with many others in Arizona, is subject to snow melt and heavy rains. Most of the time water is pooled in the bathtub itself, making a descent to the bathtub worthwhile.

When you come back to the top again, continue west on the Devil's Bathtub trail for .6 mile to where it intersects with Manning Camp Trail. A right turn here and, in only one mile, you will arrive at Manning Camp itself.

REQUIREMENTS: Half hour hiking time one way; water, food, raingear

LOCATION: East end of Rincon Mountains; Saguaro National Monument East

DIFFICULTY: Easy to moderate

ELEVATIONS: 7600' to 7480'

LENGTH: 1.2 miles one way

MAPS REQUIRED: Mica Mountain Quadrangle; 7.5 minute series topographic Pima County.

PERMIT: No, unless camping overnight; permit available at Saguaro National Monument East.

WATER: Not when very dry

INFORMATION: Storms gather quickly here

ATTRACTION: 50-foot waterfall in season

DEVIL'S BATHTUB TRAIL

HARD SURFACE

LIGHT DUTY

UNIMPROVED

TRAIL

RAILROAD

FOOT BRIDGE

BUILDINGS

WATER TANK

CAMPSITE

WINDMILL

x5290 ELEVATION CHECK

MINESHAFT

SPRING

RIM

CORRAL

PEAK

TRAILHEAD

P. PARKING

WATER

RIVER

DRAINAGE

SCALE = 1 MILE

NORTH

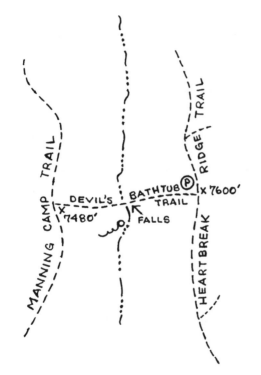

MANNING CAMP TRAIL

DEVIL'S BATHTUB TRAIL

RIDGE TRAIL

x 7600'

x 7480'

FALLS

HEARTBREAK

WINTER SPRING SUMMER FALL

HAPPY VALLEY LOOKOUT TRAIL

Saguaro National Monument East — (602) 296-8576

DIRECTION: Heartbreak Ridge Trail to peak of Happy Valley Lookout

Trailhead is ¼ mile north of intersection of Miller Creek Trail and Heartbreak Ridge Trail, on Heartbreak Ridge Trail.

The trail starts out via switchbacks right away, but the switchbacks are long and gentle. There is only about 150 feet of altitude gain on this trail, but what a difference it makes in the view from the top.

It is a great place to gaze away in any direction you choose. An awesome view of Rincon Peak awaits you.

Also on the summit is a fire watch cabin (not tower) used for forest fire monitoring during the fire season.

REQUIREMENTS: Three-quarter hour hiking time round trip; water

LOCATION: East end of Rincon Mountains; Saguaro National Monument East

DIFFICULTY: Easy

ELEVATIONS: 7200′ to 7348′

LENGTH: .2 mile one way

MAPS REQUIRED: Mica Mountain Quadrangle; 7.5 minute series topographic Pima County.

PERMIT: No, unless camping overnight; available from Saguaro National Monument East.

WATER: No

INFORMATION: Summer storms gather quickly here

ATTRACTION: Magnificent vistas.

HAPPY VALLEY
LOOKOUT TRAIL

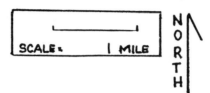

SCALE = | MILE

N
O
R
T
H

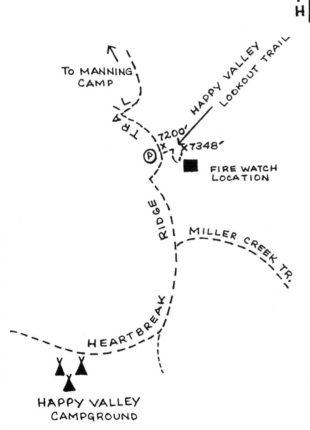

To MANNING CAMP

HAPPY VALLEY LOOKOUT TRAIL

TRAIL

7200'
x
x7348'

FIRE WATCH
LOCATION

RIDGE

MILLER CREEK TR.

HEARTBREAK

HAPPY VALLEY
CAMPGROUND

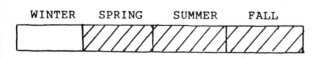

WINTER	SPRING	SUMMER	FALL

LEGEND

HARD SURFACE

LIGHT DUTY

UNIMPROVED

TRAIL

RAILROAD

FOOT BRIDGE

BUILDINGS

WATER TANK

CAMPSITE

WINDMILL

x5290
ELEVATION CHECK

MINESHAFT

SPRING

RIM

CORRAL

PEAK

TRAILHEAD

P.
PARKING

WATER

RIVER

DRAINAGE

RINCON CREEK TRAIL
Saguaro National Monument East — (602) 296-8576

DIRECTION: Happy Valley Campground to Madrona Ranger Station

Trailhead begins out of west end of Happy Valley Campground. The sign for Madrona will direct you across small creek drainage.

After you cross a small creek drainage, the trail climbs for only a very short distance before starting to drop onto the right bank of a ravine which you will follow (for some distance).

Another nice view of Rincon Peak and the surrounding hillside on the opposite side of the ravine will keep your curiosity aroused on this trail. Be sure to stop and turn around to your left and look for many waterfalls if you are hiking during a wet spell. Views of Rincon Valley and on to Tucson open up in front of you, as you slowly switchback your way lower into the ravine.

Soon you will travel a bit northwest for only a short time and then you will head west again, but not before you reach the headwaters of Rincon Creek itself. You will be looking down to the creek from about 150 feet above. I found this to be geologically interesting all the way.

At about six miles, after losing a lot of altitude, you come to a sign indicating Madrona as a right turn. *You must not continue straight here, as it is private property with no outlet. The trail to Madrona is faint and care must be taken to follow it.* In just two more miles you will arrive at Madrona Ranger Station.

Be advised that you have now traveled eight miles, and there exists no way out of the monument from Madrona Ranger Station except to return the way you came. *This is private property and there is no camping at Madrona.* The closest over-night camping is at Grass Shack Campground, five more miles north out of Madrona via Manning Camp Trail. One must consider this before attempting Rincon Creek Trail.

(continued on page 106)

RINCON CREEK TRAIL

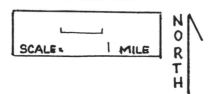

SCALE = 1 MILE

NORTH

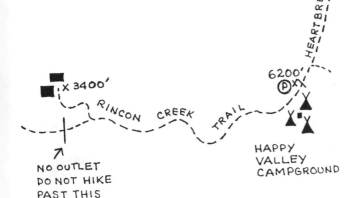

HEARTBREAK RIDGE TR.

x 3400'

RINCON CREEK TRAIL

6200'
Ⓟ XX

HAPPY VALLEY CAMPGROUND

NO OUTLET
DO NOT HIKE
PAST THIS
POINT

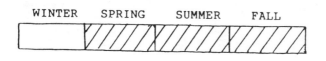

| WINTER | SPRING | SUMMER | FALL |

LEGEND

HARD SURFACE

LIGHT DUTY

UNIMPROVED TRAIL

RAILROAD

FOOT BRIDGE

BUILDINGS

WATER TANK

CAMPSITE

WINDMILL

x5290 ELEVATION CHECK

MINESHAFT

SPRING

RIM

CORRAL

PEAK

Ⓟ TRAILHEAD

P. PARKING

WATER

RIVER

DRAINAGE

REQUIREMENTS: 4-5 hours hiking time one way; water, food, raingear

LOCATION: South-central area of Rincon Mountains; Saguaro National Monument East

DIFFICULTY: Moderate

ELEVATIONS: 6200′ to 3400′

LENGTH: 8 miles one way

MAPS REQUIRED: Mica Mountain Quadrangle; 7.5 minute series topographic Pima County.

PERMIT: No, unless camping overnight; available at Saguaro National Monument East.

WATER: No

INFORMATION: Summer storms gather quickly here

ATTRACTION: Attractive geological area at headwaters of the Rincon Creek

View of Rincon Peak from Rincon Creek Trail

Peak cannot be seen from Rincon Peak Trail

Scene from Devil's Bathtub Trail

RINCON PEAK TRAIL

Saguaro National Monument East — (602) 296-8576

DIRECTION: Trailhead at Happy Valley Campground to peak

Trailhead is only 100 yards outside of Happy Valley Campground on Heartbreak Ridge Trail and is very well marked.

As this trail starts out with only small altitude changes and only a few moderate switchbacks, and even some flat areas, you would not dream of what awaits you later on the trail. You will be taken in by the vast canopy above, as well as the sunny areas.

At about .8 mile from the top, this trail turns into a back breaker with exceptionally steep switchbacks, along with endless loose rocks. These keep some hikers from attaining the honor of making it to the top. Equestrian use is out of the question on this trail.

After passing through some aspens, the reward of the trail is just ahead. Only 500 feet more of trail will afford you the view from the summit itself.

Notice the rock on which you stand and consider all the scars from lightning bolts. Do not linger on this summit.

Do not attempt this trail if you're not in shape.

REQUIREMENTS: 6 hours hiking time round trip; water, food, raingear

LOCATION: East end of Rincon Mountains; Saguaro National Monument East

DIFFICULTY: Very difficult

ELEVATIONS: 6090′ to 8482′

LENGTH: 3.2 miles one way

MAPS REQUIRED: Mica Mountain & Rincon Peak Quadrangles; 7.5 minute series topographic Pima County.

PERMIT: No, unless camping overnight; available from Saguaro National Monument East.

WATER: Not dependable

INFORMATION: *Vacate peak if storm is building*

ATTRACTION: Magnificent 360-degree vistas.

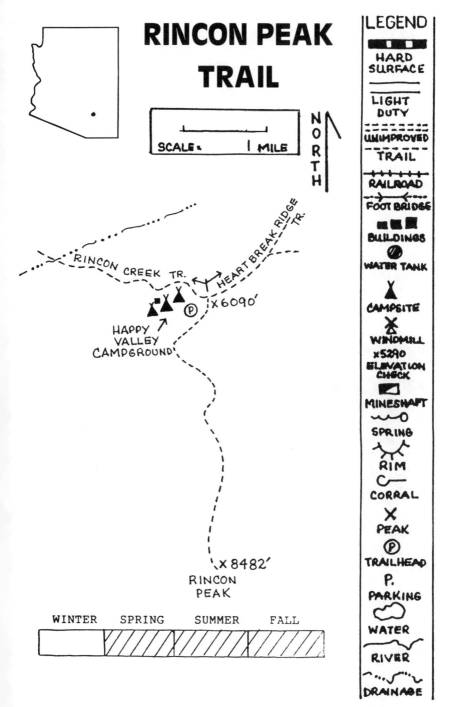

RINCON PEAK TRAIL

SCALE: 1 MILE

NORTH

RINCON CREEK TR.

HEART BREAK RIDGE TR.

x 6090'

HAPPY VALLEY CAMPGROUND

x 8482'
RINCON PEAK

WINTER | SPRING | SUMMER | FALL

LEGEND

HARD SURFACE

LIGHT DUTY

UNIMPROVED TRAIL

RAILROAD

FOOT BRIDGE

BUILDINGS

WATER TANK

CAMPSITE

WINDMILL

x5290 ELEVATION CHECK

MINESHAFT

SPRING

RIM

CORRAL

PEAK

TRAILHEAD

P. PARKING

WATER

RIVER

DRAINAGE

HEARTBREAK RIDGE TRAIL

Saguaro National Monument East — (602) 296-8576

DIRECTION: Intersection of Fire Loop Trail and Heartbreak Ridge to Happy Valley Campground

Trailhead is .7 mile east of Manning Camp on Fire Loop Trail. Heartbreak Ridge Trail heads to the southeast and downhill constantly through an area that is very rocky so, naturally, there are fewer trees. There are lots of trail bars making trail easy to follow.

In .7 mile, you come by a trail to your left called Switchback Trail. From here, continue straight south for .5 mile to the Four Corners area. This is where East Slope Trail and Devil's Bathtub Trail intersect. Again, continue straight for .5 mile to intersection where Deerhead Spring Trail comes down from the north.

From here, you encounter some gentle switchbacks and lose some altitude before you are on the ridge the trail is named for. The ridge affords magnificent views and only gentle ups and downs as you follow a true ridge.

Just before three more miles, you encounter another trail on your left called Happy Valley Lookout Trail (only .2 mile to peak). Continue straight again. In about .6 mile more, another trail comes in from the left called Miller Creek Trail. Again continue straight for .5 mile and the end of the trail at Happy Valley Campground.

REQUIREMENTS: 3 hours hiking time one way; water food, raingear

LOCATION: East end of Rincon Mountains; Saguaro National Monument East

DIFFICULTY: Easy to moderate

ELEVATIONS: 7940' to 6200'

LENGTH: 5.7 miles one way

(continued on page 112)

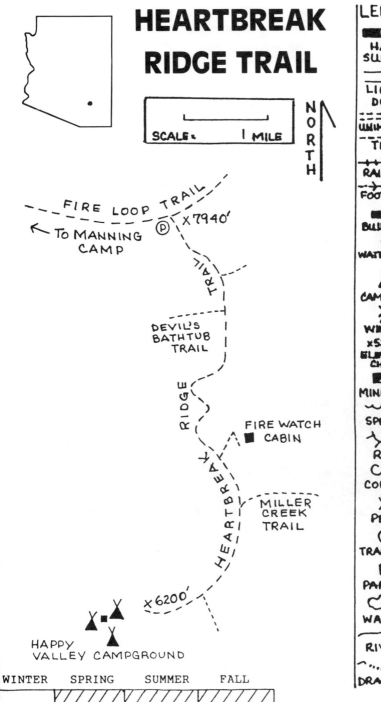

HEARTBREAK RIDGE TRAIL

NORTH

SCALE: 1 MILE

FIRE LOOP TRAIL

← TO MANNING CAMP

(P) X 7940'

TRAIL

DEVIL'S BATHTUB TRAIL

RIDGE

FIRE WATCH CABIN

HEARTBREAK

MILLER CREEK TRAIL

X 6200'

HAPPY VALLEY CAMPGROUND

WINTER	SPRING	SUMMER	FALL

LEGEND

HARD SURFACE

LIGHT DUTY

UNIMPROVED TRAIL

RAILROAD

FOOT BRIDGE

BUILDINGS

WATER TANK

CAMPSITE

WINDMILL

x5290 ELEVATION CHECK

MINESHAFT

SPRING

RIM

CORRAL

PEAK

(P) TRAILHEAD

P. PARKING

WATER

RIVER

DRAINAGE

MAPS REQUIRED: Mica Mountain Quadrangle; 7.5 minute series topographic Pima County.

PERMIT: No, unless camping overnight; available from Saguaro National Monument East.

WATER: No

INFORMATION: *Trail follows summit ridge; beware of violent summer storms.*

ATTRACTION: Allows Happy Valley Lookout side trip; magnificent vistas.

Descending from ridge on Heartbreak Ridge Trail

Mighty aspens on Aspen Loop Trail

Looking up, halfway up Turkey Creek Trail

ASPEN LOOP TRAIL

Santa Catalina Ranger District — (602) 749-8700

DIRECTION: Marshall Gulch Campground to Marshall Saddle and back to campground via loop

High above Tucson on Mt. Lemmon Highway, you will come to a fork in the road leading to Ski Valley on the right, and through the tiny village of Summerhaven to the left. Take the left fork.

In another mile, you will arrive at Marshall Gulch Picnic Area. The trailhead is marked by a sign in the campground.

About 300 feet into the trail, you will see a fork; travel to the right uphill. After one-half mile, you will encounter switchbacks firmly placed in a mighty aspen grove.

At about 1.5 miles, the switchbacks give way to level ground and another fork is encountered. A turn to the left takes you to Lunch Ledge, but your direction of travel should be to the right to Marshall Saddle at 2.4 miles and the highest point at 8,200 feet. At this sunny area, four trails converge. You should take the trail indicated on the signs as "Marshall Gulch 1.2 miles."

At just over 3.5 miles, you will find yourself where you started.

REQUIREMENTS: 4-5 hours hiking time round trip; water, snack, raingear

LOCATION: Marshall Gulch Picnic Area; Santa Catalina Mountains

DIFFICULTY: Moderate

ELEVATIONS: 7410' to 8400'

LENGTH: 3.8 miles round trip

MAPS REQUIRED: Mt. Lemmon Quadrangle; 7.5 minute series topographic Pima County.

PERMIT: No

WATER: Not dependable

INFORMATION: Area subject to severe summer storms

ATTRACTION: Attractive area with aspens.

ASPEN LOOP
TRAIL

SCALE: 1 MILE

NORTH

↑ TO SUMMERHAVEN

x 8400

PICNIC AREA

7410 x

ASPEN TRAIL

WINTER	SPRING	SUMMER	FALL
	///////	////////	////////

TURKEY CREEK TRAIL

Saguaro National Monument East — (602) 296-8576

DIRECTION: Trailhead to intersection with Deerhead Spring Trail

To reach Turkey Creek Trailhead, take the Mescal, J-six Ranch exit (No. 297) off I-10 and turn north on USFS Route 35. After 16.4 miles north of the interstate, just past a sign for Miller Creek Trail, there will be a small sign on your left indicating USFS Route 4408.

Turn left here and travel *.4 mile through a gate, which you must close,* into an area with large sycamore trees. The trailhead is at the opposite end of this area.

Do not attempt this trail unless you are in excellent shape.

The first mile and a half follows, rather steeply at times, an old jeep trail; however, it can be traversed by 4-wheel drive to the parking area. From this point, it is a foot trail as you continue to gain altitude.

At 3 miles, you come to the Saguaro National Monument East gate; *again, please close it behind you.* For the next 3 miles the trail gets very steep with what seems like an endless series of switchbacks.

Exactly 6 miles from the start, you come to Deerhead Spring and a small, 3-log foot bridge. Take time to stop on it and look to a two-o'clock position and, as you look across a small, damp meadow, you will see the remaining .2 mile (very steep) to Deerhead Spring Trail.

A right turn takes you to Spud Rock Campground in .7 mile.

REQUIREMENTS: 4 hours hiking time one way; water, food, raingear

LOCATION: East end of Rincon Mountains; Saguaro National Monument East

(continued on page 118)

TURKEY CREEK TRAIL

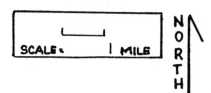

SCALE: | MILE

NORTH

LEGEND

HARD SURFACE

LIGHT DUTY

UNIMPROVED

TRAIL

RAILROAD

FOOT BRIDGE

BUILDINGS

WATER TANK

CAMPSITE

WINDMILL

x5290 ELEVATION CHECK

MINESHAFT

SPRING

RIM

CORRAL

PEAK

TRAILHEAD

P. PARKING

WATER

RIVER

DRAINAGE

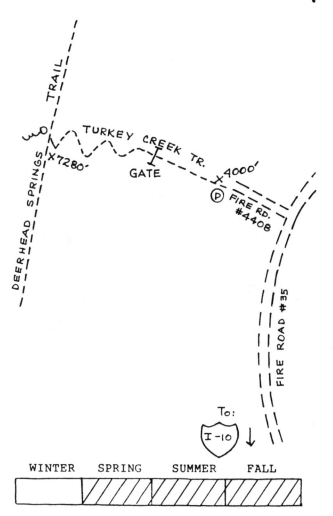

TURKEY CREEK TR.

TRAIL

DEER HEAD SPRINGS

X7280'

GATE

4000'

FIRE RD. #4408

FIRE ROAD #35

To:
I-10

| WINTER | SPRING | SUMMER | FALL |

DIFFICULTY: Very difficult

ELEVATIONS: 4000' to 7280'

LENGTH: 6.2 miles one way

MAPS REQUIRED: Mica Mountain Quadrangle; 7.5 minute series topographic Pima County.

PERMIT: No, unless camping overnight; available from Saguaro National Monument East.

WATER: No

INFORMATION: *Not a trail for a novice. Summer storms gather quickly here*

ATTRACTION: Quickest way to Spudrock Campground, Devil's Bathtub and Manning Campground.

Butterfly Trail — on way to Mt. Bigelow

Approaching Mica Mountain Trail

Climbing Miller Creek Trail

BUTTERFLY TRAIL

Santa Catalina Ranger District — (602) 749-8700

DIRECTION: Palisades Trailhead to Mt. Bigelow

The trailhead is located about 36 miles northeast of Tucson on the Mt. Lemmon Highway, just across the road from the Palisades Ranger Station.

The trail starts gently and remains so, even though you encounter switchbacks along the way. About one-half mile from the trailhead, you will come to a ridge where three more trails meet the one you're on. The trails are: Kragge Trail Overlook, Kellogg Mountain and the continuation of Butterfly Trail to Soldier Camp.

Turn left here and continue for another half mile, via gentle switchbacks, to the summit of Mt. Bigelow. There are many good views of Tucson and the valley below and also a fire tower on the summit.

REQUIREMENTS: 1.5 hours hiking time round trip; water, food or snacks

LOCATION: At Palisades Ranger Station, 36 miles northeast of Tucson on Mt. Lemmon Highway

DIFFICULTY: Easy

ELEVATIONS: 7950' to 8550'

LENGTH: 1 mile one way

MAPS REQUIRED: Mt. Lemmon Quadrangle; 7.5 minute series topographic Pima County.

PERMIT: No

WATER: No

INFORMATION: Be aware of fast-moving summer storms

ATTRACTION: Magnificent views of Tucson and valley below.

BUTTERFLY TRAIL

SCALE = ½ MILE

NORTH

LEGEND

- ▬ ▬ ▬ HARD SURFACE
- ───── LIGHT DUTY
- ═══ UNIMPROVED
- ─ ─ ─ TRAIL
- ┼┼┼┼ RAILROAD
- ─►─◄─ FOOT BRIDGE
- ▪ ▪ ■ BUILDINGS
- ⊘ WATER TANK
- ⛺ CAMPSITE
- ✕ WINDMILL
- x5290 ELEVATION CHECK
- ▭ MINESHAFT
- ∿o SPRING
- ☼ RIM
- C CORRAL
- ✕ PEAK
- Ⓟ TRAILHEAD
- P. PARKING
- ⌁ WATER
- ∿ RIVER
- ∿ DRAINAGE

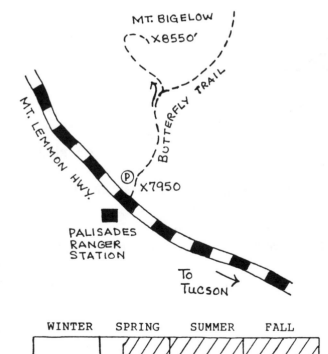

MT. BIGELOW
X8550'

BUTTERFLY TRAIL

MT. LEMMON HWY.

Ⓟ X7950

PALISADES RANGER STATION

To TUCSON

WINTER	SPRING	SUMMER	FALL

PIMA COUNTY

MICA MOUNTAIN TRAIL

Saguaro National Monument East — (602) 296-8576

DIRECTION: Manning Camp to Mica Mountain Peak

Just north of Manning Camp cabin is a signed trail called Fire Loop Trail, which directs you to Mica Fire Tower. You are on the trail for only .1 mile before you encounter your first intersection and another sign directing you to continue on Mica Mountain Trail to reach the peak.

At .6 mile, you come to another fork in the trail where Mica Meadow Trail veers right. Be sure to continue straight on Mica Mountain Trail. Only .1 mile further is yet another fork where Spud Rock Trail veers left. Again continue straight on Mica Mountain Trail for .7 mile.

The trail dead ends into Fire Loop Trail. A left turn here, and a distance of only .1 mile will bring you to the peak and to where Mica Fire Tower used to stand.

REQUIREMENTS: 2 hours hiking time round trip; food, water, raingear

LOCATION: Saguaro National Monument East

DIFFICULTY: Easy

ELEVATIONS: 8000' to 8666'

LENGTH: 1¾ miles one way

MAPS REQUIRED: Mica Mountain Quadrangle; 7.5 minute series topographic Pima County.

PERMIT: No, unless camping overnight; available from Saguaro National Monument East.

WATER: Manning Camp (dependable)

INFORMATION: Permit available from Saguaro National Monument East

ATTRACTION: Highest peak in the Rincon Mountains

MICA MOUNTAIN TRAIL

SCALE: 1 MILE

NORTH

LEGEND

HARD SURFACE

LIGHT DUTY

UNIMPROVED

TRAIL

RAILROAD

FOOT BRIDGE

BUILDINGS

WATER TANK

CAMPSITE

WINDMILL

x5290 **ELEVATION CHECK**

MINESHAFT

SPRING

RIM

CORRAL

X **PEAK**

Ⓟ **TRAILHEAD**

P. **PARKING**

WATER

RIVER

DRAINAGE

FIRE LOOP TRAIL

X 8666' MICA MTN.

SPUD ROCK TRAIL

MICA MOUNTAIN TRAIL

MICA MEADOW TRAIL

COWHEAD SADDLE TR.

MANNING CAMP TR.

HEARTBREAK RIDGE TR.

Ⓟ

X 8000' MANNING CAMP

WINTER   SPRING   SUMMER   FALL

Mica Mountain Trail / 123

MILLER CREEK TRAIL

Saguaro National Monument East — (602) 296-8576

DIRECTION: Trailhead to intersection with Heartbreak Ridge Trail

To reach Miller Creek Trailhead, travel southeast of Tucson on I-10 to the Mescal Exit 297, turning onto USFWS Route #35. Take the gravel road 16 miles north to a sign that reads, "Miller Creek Trailhead." Turn left and continue only .2 mile more to the trailhead.

The trail is evident as you pass through a gate that you are asked to close behind you. After ¾ mile, you start to switchback out of the left side of Miller Canyon, as well as across several drainages. In another ¾ mile, you will arrive at the well-marked entry to Saguaro National Monument East.

Now the trail becomes a bit more steep and the switch-backs continue. At about 4.4 miles from the start, Miller Creek Trail runs into Heartbreak Ridge Trail. An impressive view of Rincon Peak at 8,482 feet is to be seen on your left from this point.

If you continue left here on Heartbreak Ridge Trail, you will encounter Happy Valley Campground and Rincon Peak Trail.

REQUIREMENTS: 5 hours hiking time round trip; water food, raingear

LOCATION: Saguaro National Monument East

DIFFICULTY: Difficult

ELEVATIONS: 4200′ to 6120′

LENGTH: 4.4 miles one way

MAPS REQUIRED: Mica Mountain Quadrangle; 7.5 minute series topographic Pima County.

PERMIT: If you camp overnight

WATER: Not dependable

INFORMATION: Camping permit available from Saguaro National Monument East

ATTRACTION: Shortest route to Happy Valley Campground and Rincon Peak Trail.

MILLER CREEK TRAIL

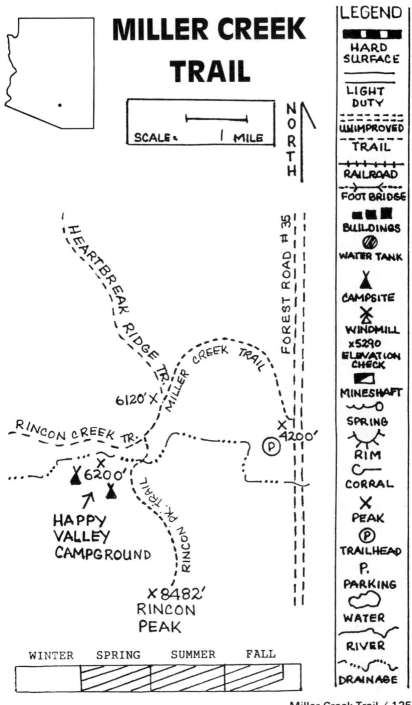

SCALE = 1 MILE

NORTH

LEGEND

HARD SURFACE

LIGHT DUTY

UNIMPROVED

TRAIL

RAILROAD

FOOT BRIDGE

BUILDINGS

WATER TANK

CAMPSITE

WINDMILL

x5290 ELEVATION CHECK

MINESHAFT

SPRING

RIM

CORRAL

PEAK

TRAILHEAD

P. PARKING

WATER

RIVER

DRAINAGE

HEARTBREAK RIDGE TR.

MILLER CREEK TRAIL

FOREST ROAD # 35

6120' X

RINCON CREEK TR.

X 4200'

P

X 6200'

HAPPY VALLEY CAMPGROUND

RINCON PK. TRAIL

X 8482' RINCON PEAK

WINTER   SPRING   SUMMER   FALL

BEAR CANYON TRAIL

Santa Catalina Ranger District — (602) 749-8700

DIRECTION: Trailhead to a series of seven waterfalls

To get to Sabino Canyon Visitor's Center, take I-10 south to Tucson. As you come into north Tucson, travel east on Ina Road and, after crossing First Avenue, make a right turn on Skyline Drive and a second right turn on Sunrise Drive, then a left turn on Sabino Canyon Road to the center. Make arrangements at the information booth to be trammed to the trailhead.

The trail is spacious and well-kept. It skirts Bear Creek all the way. You will cross the creek many times via hand-built stepping stones.

High, massive cliffs close in on you on both sides as you come to some gentle switchbacks at 1½ miles. Then for one-half mile, you hike about 100 feet above the creek. Very nice views of the canyon.

At two miles you will come to a fork in the trail. Stay left for only .2 mile and you will come to the falls themselves across the creek. The falls only flow during the rainy part of winter and in July and August during the monsoon season.

REQUIREMENTS: 3 hours hiking time round trip; water, snack

LOCATION: Sabino Canyon; Catalina Mountains

DIFFICULTY: Easy

ELEVATIONS: 2800' to 3200'

LENGTH: 2.2 miles one way

MAPS REQUIRED: Sabino Canyon Quadrangle; 7.5 minute series topographic Pima County.

PERMIT: No

WATER: Not dependable

INFORMATION: Very hot in summer; falls are not always flowing

ATTRACTION: Very peaceful riparian area.

BEAR CANYON TRAIL

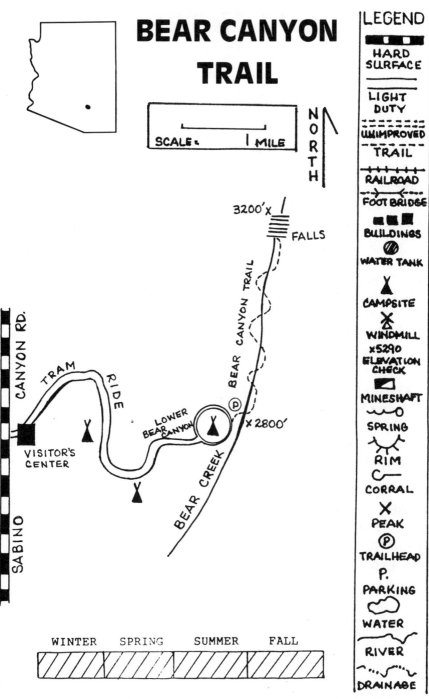

LEGEND

HARD SURFACE

LIGHT DUTY

UNIMPROVED TRAIL

RAILROAD

FOOT BRIDGE

BUILDINGS

WATER TANK

CAMPSITE

WINDMILL

x5290 ELEVATION CHECK

MINESHAFT

SPRING

RIM

CORRAL

PEAK

Ⓟ TRAILHEAD

P. PARKING

WATER

RIVER

DRAINAGE

SCALE = 1 MILE

NORTH

3200'x

FALLS

BEAR CANYON TRAIL

CANYON RD.

TRAM RIDE

LOWER BEAR CANYON

Ⓟ

x 2800'

VISITOR'S CENTER

BEAR CREEK

SABINO

WINTER   SPRING   SUMMER   FALL

HUNTER TRAIL

Picacho Peak State Park — (602) 466-3183

DIRECTION: Trailhead to Picacho Peak

Picacho Peak State Park is located about halfway between Phoenix and Tucson. The trail begins at the parking area near Saguaro Ramada on Barrett Loop Drive. This trail has a lot of hard elevation gain.

Hikers ascend the north slope to the upper saddle (approximately one mile). A series of 15 iron posts and cables (four on the north slope, 11 on the south) are placed in spots where hikers cross bedrock or where the pitch is very steep.

The trail descends as you head around to the south side, losing altitude rapidly, almost all that you have gained. The back side is difficult, but the sense of adventure will fuel you with what is needed for the steep ascent and your many steps over metal-edged planks laid on horizontal iron bars driven into rock faces.

"See you at the top" takes on a whole new meaning here.

REQUIREMENTS: 4-5 hours hiking time round trip; water, sturdy shoes, gloves

LOCATION: Picacho State Park

DIFFICULTY: Very difficult

ELEVATIONS: 2000′ to 3374′

LENGTH: 2 miles one way

MAPS REQUIRED: Newman Park Quadrangle; 7.5 minute series topographic Pinal County.

PERMIT: No

WATER: No

INFORMATION: Must check in at visitor's center; a small fee is charged.

ATTRACTION: Breathtaking 360° view.

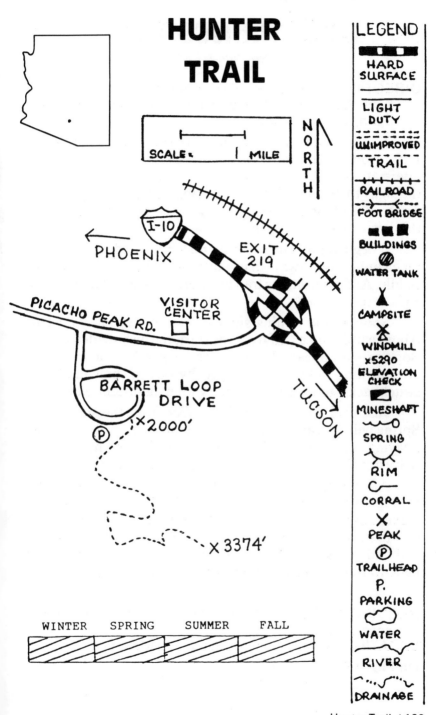

HUNTER TRAIL

SCALE = 1 MILE

NORTH

I-10

← PHOENIX

EXIT 219

PICACHO PEAK RD.

VISITOR CENTER

BARRETT LOOP DRIVE

TUCSON

Ⓟ

×2000'

×3374'

WINTER	SPRING	SUMMER	FALL

LEGEND

▬ HARD SURFACE

— LIGHT DUTY

╌╌╌ UNIMPROVED TRAIL

┼┼┼ RAILROAD

⇢⇠ FOOT BRIDGE

■■■ BUILDINGS

⊘ WATER TANK

⛺ CAMPSITE

✗ WINDMILL

×5290 ELEVATION CHECK

◪ MINESHAFT

∿o SPRING

RIM

⌒ CORRAL

✗ PEAK

Ⓟ TRAILHEAD

P. PARKING

WATER

RIVER

DRAINAGE

BOG SPRINGS TRAIL

Nogales Ranger District — (602) 281-2296

DIRECTION: Bog Springs Campground to Bog Springs, to Kent Spring, to Sylvester Spring, via loop back to Bog Springs Campground

To reach Madera Canyon, drive south from Tucson on I-19. About four miles south of Green Valley, exit the interstate onto Continental/Madera Canyon Road. Follow the signs to Madera Canyon and Bog Springs Campground. The trailhead for the hike to Bog Springs is found just past the third campsite on the right.

It begins as an old jeep trail, no longer used, and is pretty much uphill right away. In just over one-half mile, you reach a saddle. At this point, the trail takes off to the left. The jeep trail ends here.

Soon an old mining site comes into view on your left. About a mile and a half from the start, the lush shaded area of Bog Springs appears. Next, you travel gently up a draw and, after turning right, climb steeply, by way of some moderate switchbacks, to a welcome ridge with magnificent views.

Just over two and one-half miles from the start, Kent Spring will appear. It's not as shaded but usually dependable. Leaving here, you quickly lose altitude for one-half mile to Sylvester Spring, the least impressive of the three.

After climbing a draw on your left and dropping down through a drainage ditch leading to Madera Creek, the trail makes its way to a fork. Although there are no signs, you must stay to the right and, at just over four miles from the start, you will find yourself back at the saddle. Turn right and continue back to Bog Springs Campground via the old jeep trail.

REQUIREMENTS: 3-4 hours hiking time round trip; water snack, raingear

LOCATION: Madera Canyon, Santa Rita Mountains

DIFFICULTY: Moderate

(continued on page 132)

BOG SPRINGS
TRAIL

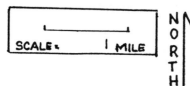

SCALE = | MILE

NORTH

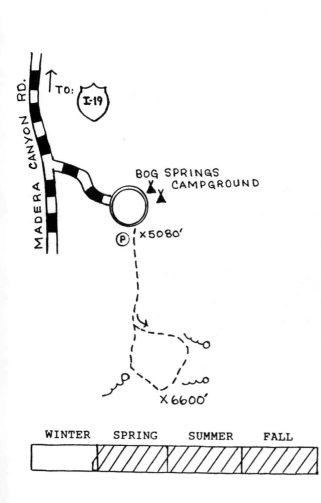

MADERA CANYON RD.

↑ TO: I-19

BOG SPRINGS
CAMPGROUND

Ⓟ ×5080'

×6600'

| WINTER | SPRING | SUMMER | FALL |

LEGEND

HARD SURFACE

LIGHT DUTY

UNIMPROVED TRAIL

RAILROAD

FOOT BRIDGE

BUILDINGS

WATER TANK

CAMPSITE

WINDMILL

×5290 ELEVATION CHECK

MINESHAFT

SPRING

RIM

CORRAL

PEAK

Ⓟ TRAILHEAD

P. PARKING

WATER

RIVER

DRAINAGE

ELEVATIONS: 5080′ to 6600′

LENGTH: 4.5 miles one way

MAPS REQUIRED: Mt. Wrightson Quadrangle; 7.5 minute series topographic Santa Cruz County.

PERMIT: No

WATER: Not always dependable at springs.

INFORMATION: Area subject to severe summer storms

ATTRACTION: Views of surrounding lowlands and the fantastic Mt. Wrightson

View from Bog Springs Trail

Author on steep backside of Hunter Trail

One of seven falls of Bear Canyon Falls

SUPER TRAIL

Nogales Ranger District — (602) 281-2296

DIRECTION: Roundup Campground Trailhead to Peak

Travel South of Tucson on I-19 and exit at the Continental turnoff (#63). After a left turn here, watch for another left turn onto White House Canyon Road. Twelve miles later, turn off onto Madera Canyon Road and park at Roundup Campground picnic area. Trail leaves the parking area along a drainage.

The trail from here continues 8.1 miles to the top with its relentless 8% grade. Trail difficulty is rated as fair, but at times seems much worse, as there is no letup in the grade anywhere.

At the halfway point, you will arrive at "Josephine Saddle" where four trails converge. Continue on Super Trail. From this point on, the trail switchbacks become more numerous to Baldy Saddle at 7.1 miles. To this point you will have traversed about 75 switchbacks.

The last mile now to the top gets much steeper, with about 39 more switchbacks, so pace yourself; you're almost there. *Altitude sickness can set in easily here.*

On a clear day, the Gulf of California can be seen from the rounded peak of only 50 feet by 200 feet.

REQUIREMENTS: 8-9 hours hiking time round trip; water food, raingear, warm clothes

LOCATION: 38 miles south of Tucson

DIFFICULTY: Difficult

ELEVATIONS: 5440' to 9453'

LENGTH: 8.1 miles one way

MAPS REQUIRED: Mt. Wrightson Quadrangle; 15 minute series topographic Santa Cruz County.

PERMIT: No

WATER: Three springs, not dependable

INFORMATION: Weather unpredictable on summit

ATTRACTION: Fantastic views. Birders paradise

SUPER
TRAIL

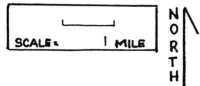

SCALE: 1 MILE

NORTH

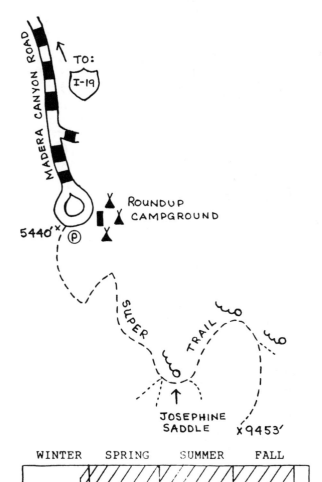

MADERA CANYON ROAD

TO: I-19

ROUNDUP CAMPGROUND

5440'x P

SUPER TRAIL

JOSEPHINE SADDLE

X9453'

WINTER	SPRING	SUMMER	FALL

LEGEND

HARD SURFACE

LIGHT DUTY

UNIMPROVED TRAIL

RAILROAD

FOOT BRIDGE

BUILDINGS

WATER TANK

CAMPSITE

WINDMILL

x5290 ELEVATION CHECK

MINESHAFT

SPRING

RIM

CORRAL

X PEAK

P TRAILHEAD

P. PARKING

WATER

RIVER

DRAINAGE

HIGHLINE
REFERENCE MAP

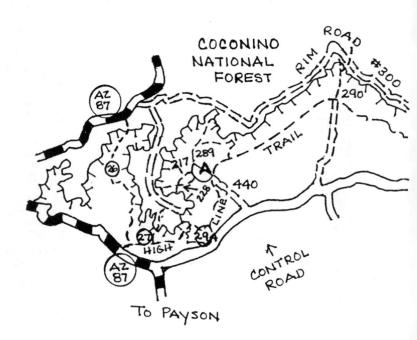

Trail Index

TRAIL

PAYSON RANGER DIST.

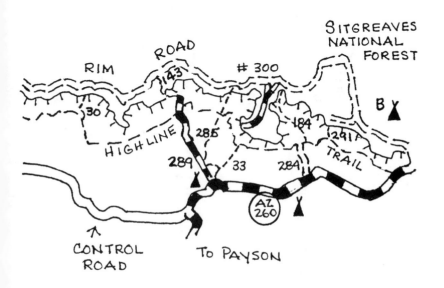

Trail Index

30 Myrtle
#143 Babe Haught
#285 Horton Creek
$292 Horton Spring
#278 Promontory Butte
33 Derrick/Spur
#184 See Canyon
#291 Drew

B Woods Canyon Lake

CHIRICAHUA NATIONAL MONUMENT
REFERENCE MAP

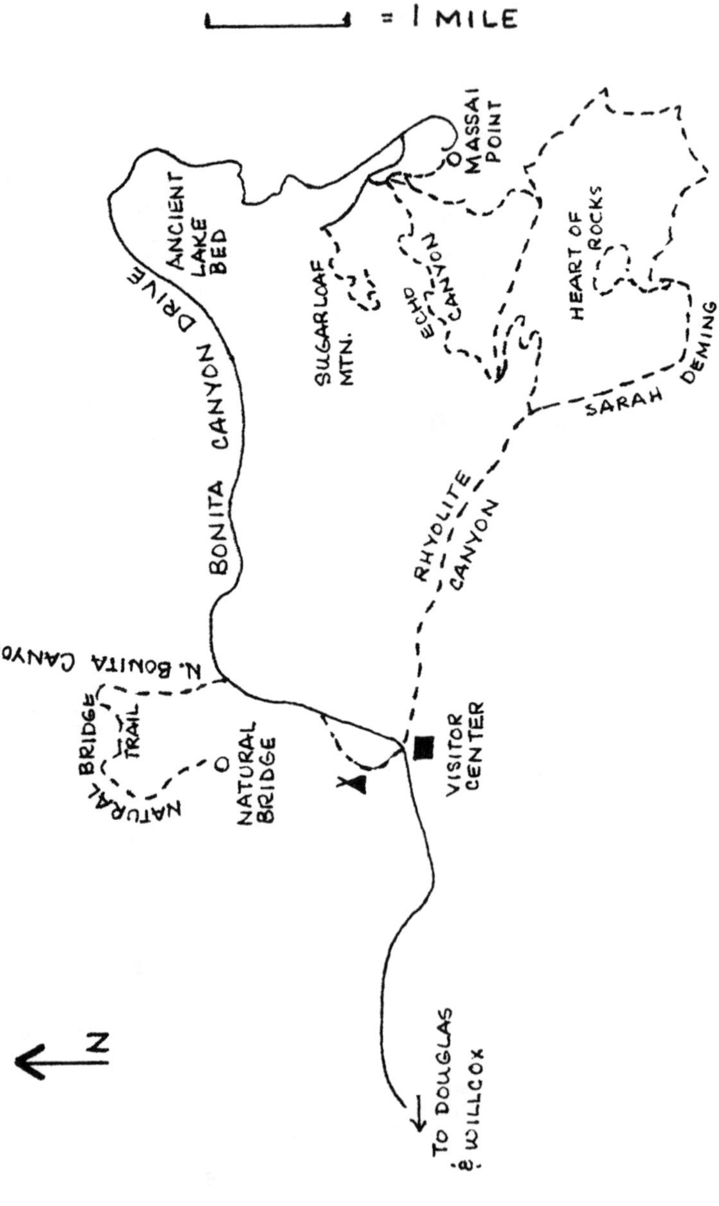

⊢———⊣ = 1 MILE

MASSAI POINT

ANCIENT LAKE BED

SUGARLOAF MTN.

ECHO CANYON

HEART OF ROCKS

DEMING

SARAH

RHYOLITE CANYON

BONITA CANYON DRIVE

N. BONITA CANYON

BRIDGE TRAIL

NATURAL BRIDGE

NATURAL BRIDGE

VISITOR CENTER

← N

TO DOUGLAS & WILLCOX

RINCON WILDERNESS

SAGUARO NATIONAL MONUMENT

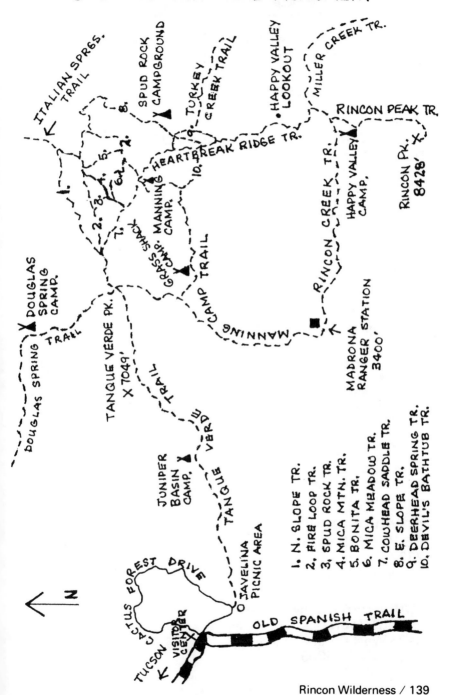

1. N. SLOPE TR.
2. FIRE LOOP TR.
3. SPUD ROCK TR.
4. MICA MTN. TR.
5. BONITA TR.
6. MICA MEADOW TR.
7. COWHEAD SADDLE TR.
8. E. SLOPE TR.
9. DEERHEAD SPRING TR.
10. DEVIL'S BATHTUB TR.

Where to obtain additional
INFORMATION
on the trails in this book

SPRINGERVILLE RANGER DISTRICT
P.O. Box 640
Springerville, AZ 85938   602-333-4372
    West Fork Trail
    South Fork Trail

CHIRICAHUA NATIONAL MONUMENT
Dos Cabezas Route
Box 6500
Willcox, AZ 85643   602-824-3560
    Echo Canyon Trail
    Sugarloaf Mountain Trail
    Natural Bridge Trail
    Rhyolite/Sara Deming Trail

WILLIAMS RANGER DISTRICT
Route 1, Box 142
Williams, AZ 86046   602-635-2633
    Bill Williams Trail

PAYSON RANGER DISTRICT
1009 East Highway 260
Payson, AZ 85541   602-474-2269

Turkey Spring Trail	Derrick Trail
See Canyon Trail	West Webber Trail
Myrtle Trail	Milk Ranch Point West Trail
Donahue Trail	Railroad Tunnel Trail
Babe Haught Trail	Col. Devon Trail
Pine Canyon Trail	Promontory Butte Trail
Horton Creek Trail	Red Rock Trail
Drew Trail	Horton Spring Trail
East Webber Trail	Barnhardt Trail
Derrick Spur Trail	Shake Tree Trail

CITY OF PHOENIX PARKS,
RECREATION and LIBRARY DEPARTMENT
2333 N. Central Ave.
Phoenix, AZ 85004   602-262-4986
    Hidden Valley Trail

MARICOPA COUNTY PARKS and RECREATION
DEPARTMENT
3475 West Durango Street
Phoenix, AZ 85009   602-272-8871
    Waterfall Trail

SAGUARO NATIONAL MONUMENT EAST
3693 South Old Spanish Trail
Tucson, AZ 85730   602-296-8576
> Bonita Trail
> Mica Mountain Trail
> Devil's Bathtub Trail
> Happy Valley Lookout Trail
> Rincon Creek Trail
> Rincon Peak Trail
> Heartbreak Ridge Trail
> Turkey Creek Trail
> Mica Mountain Trail
> Miller Creek Trail

PICACHO PEAK STATE PARK
P.O. Box 275
Picacho, AZ 85241   602-466-3183
> Hunter Trail

SANTA CATALINA RANGER DISTRICT
5700 N. Sabino Canyon Rd.
Tucson, AZ 85715   602-749-8700
> Butterfly Trail
> Bear Canyon Trail
> Aspen Loop Trail

NOGALES RANGER DISTRICT
2251 N. Grand Ave.
Nogales, AZ 85621   602-281-2296
> Bog Springs Trail
> Super Trail

PLEASANT VALLEY RANGER DISTRICT
P.O. Box 450
Young, AZ 85554   602-462-3311
> Parker Creek Trail

MESA RANGER DISTRICT
Box 5800
Mesa, AZ 85211   602-835-1161
> Hieroglyphic Trail
> Peralta Trail
> Four Peaks Trail

CHALENDER RANGER DISTRICT
501 W. Bill Williams
Williams, AZ 86046   602-635-2676
> Kendrick Mountain Trail

Trail Etiquette

Let's face it, if you meet someone on the trail, they are there to have a good time and get away from it all, the same as you. If everyone exercises courtesy and cooperation, then everyone has a better time.

Trail etiquette does not only mean using good manners toward other people, but also having respect for the trail itself and its signing.

Do not cut switchbacks on a trail, as it does cause erosion. Switchbacks are built to make a trail easier and cutting them only makes your hike harder.

Hiking up steep grades sometimes requires as much from you mentally as physically. Downhill hikers must always yield to hikers coming uphill, and do it in such a way as not to break their stride or concentration.

If you are hiking faster than the party ahead of you, slow down and wait for them to allow you to pass at an ideal location; thank them.

If you stop for a rest, do so well off the trail, in order to give others a clear path to travel. It is also easier for you not to be in their road.

Hiking or riding bikes on a wet trail ruins trails eventually, as well as cutting new trails to make shortcuts. We must respect the work that went into the original trail construction if we expect them to remain.

All trail users must yield to all trail stock. These animals are excitable, so remain calm and quiet as you allow them to pass. If these animals are panicked, a rider (or even you) could get badly hurt.

If you are allowed a pet on the trail, keep it on a leash. Be careful that you are clear of other hikers so as not to have the leash trip them.

The wilderness is a pristine, rewarding area if one will only take the time to enjoy it. I don't think anything messes it up more than loud noises or yelling for no reason.

If we all work together, we can make the great outdoors a pleasant place for everyone now, as well as in the future.

Weather -
Great but Changeable

The saying goes, "if you don't like the weather in Arizona, then just wait a few minutes."

This is a fine example of how fast a change can start to occur and, depending on how far you are out on the trail, and if unprepared, can be the start of your demise.

Arizona's wide array of extremes from the hot arid desert to the cool (if not freezing) lofty peaks carry with them the perfect ingredients for you to be concerned — concerned enough to insure that you never travel unprepared.

July and August are months that are most unpredictable, indeed. Storms gather quickly and drop a lot of water to cause real hazards in the deserts and mountains. Flash floods come in a flash and temperatures can drop severely in only minutes.

Winter rains in early spring are not to be taken lightly, either. As it is a colder time of the year, the dangers may be worse.

Check weather conditions and forecasts before you travel the trails. Many have lost their lives taking our deserts and mountains for granted.

Again I will stress, go prepared in every way you can, and be informed!

Coping with Hypothermia

Hypothermia is a condition that can set in when body heat is lost at a faster rate than your body can manufacture it.

One obvious place you may develop hypothermia is in water. Even though you are floating in a life preserver, it makes no difference. Even in 70 to 80 degree water, when exhausted, you will become unconscious in 3 to 12 hours. When in 32 degree water, the longest you would live would be 45 minutes.

In water is not the only place you can develop hypothermia, as you only need to get wet in rain, sleet, snow or heavy fog. Even perspiration, along with a moderately cool wind, can start the process. When you are wet in a moderate wind, a process the same as evaporative cooling will begin with no hope of your body keeping up.

More than half your body's heat is lost from your head and neck being exposed. Obviously, then, a good winter hat with ear tabs, along with a scarf, will do a lot to slow down your major heat loss.

Other susceptible areas are your hands and feet. It is a fact that mittens will keep your hands warmer than gloves, as the air around your hands will act as insulation. Waterproof boots will take care of your feet. Some rain gear only drapes your upper body and will soak your lower pant legs and boots. So, a better rain gear application is a two-piece coat and pants to relieve this problem.

If you find yourself in this situation, stop and make camp early and get a fire started, and try to create some cover. If you do this, you may not make it home that night and be overdue but, if you don't, you may not make it home at all. It's a small price to save your life.

It is most important to eat. Food will cause your body to develop heat from the digestion process. Fatty food, along with protein from meat or beans, creates a longer-lasting heat.

If someone in your group is showing signs of hypothermia, and you have made camp, get this person into dry clothes first of all and near your fire, if you have managed to start one. While this is being done, someone can be prewarming a sleeping bag, either at your fire or by lying down in it. Build an insulation barrier with leaves, etc., on which to lay the sleeping bag and keep him out of the wind. If the person is semiconscious, give him warm drinks.

If the patient is going into severe hypothermia, then strip him and also yourself of clothing and get into the sleeping bag with this person, as there is no faster way to convey body heat. You have no other choice than to do this; it's almost a sure bet to save a life.

When headed to the mountains, think of hypothermia. When shopping for outdoor hiking gear, think hypothermia.

Contents of Your Day Pack

Listed below are items I feel comfortable with. Feel free to add or subtract to suit your needs. Keep in mind that you may be planning a day hike that could turn into overnite for a variety of reasons. Again, go prepared!

1. Small flashlight, bulbs and batteries
2. Candies that will not melt or spoil
3. Whistle (a police whistle is ideal)
4. Good compass
5. Toilet paper
6. Complete first aid kit
7. Salt tablets
8. Strong sun screen
9. Any medicines or prescriptions you need
10. Pocket knife
11. Pencil and paper
12. Lighter and waterproof matches
13. Moleskin
14. Lip salve
15. Bug spray for body
16. One day extra food that will not spoil
17. Leakproof canteen and extra water
18. Enough clothing for possible overnight stay
19. Plastic bag for litter
20. Raingear
21. Hat
22. Gloves or mittens
23. Sunglasses
24. Maps
25. Camera and film
26. Identification

I will stress that your first aid kit and maps are valuable only if you study them very carefully **before** you leave.

If you do that and take along all of the above for your day hike, you can feel comfortable about your venture.

Let your friends or family know where you are going and when you expect to return and then stick to that plan so they can feel comfortable as well.

Contents
of your Backpack

It is obvious that a day pack list is not ample by itself for multiple day outings. Nothing can ruin your outing quicker than an ill-fitting backpack. Make sure you get one large enough to fit perfectly. When satisfied with this, transfer everything from your day pack to your backpack and add the following (Again, these are things that I am comfortable with; pack to suit yourself.):

1. **Sleeping bag and bed roll.**
    Ask your supplier for help selecting this. Ask which is best for where you hike the most during time of year you hike.

2. **Tent.**
    Make sure your tent is portable and, above all, light-weight.

3. **Camping stove and extra fuel.**
    Buy a dependable product that is lightweight. It's easier than gathering wood. You are not permitted to build a wood fire in some areas.

4. **Permits.**
    By all means, pack needed permits so you can get to them easily.

Of course, all of the advice given you at the end of the Day Pack list also applies again here.

Safety Rules
for Survival in the Desert

(Courtesy Maricopa County Civil Defense and Emergency Services)

1. Never go into the desert without first informing someone as to your destination, your route and when you will return. STICK TO YOUR PLAN.

2. Carry at least one gallon of water per person per day of your trip. Plastic jugs are handy and portable.

3. Be sure your vehicle is in good condition.

4. KEEP AN EYE ON THE SKY. Flash floods may occur any time "thunderheads" are in sight, even though it may not rain where you are.

5. If your vehicle breaks down, stay near it. Your emergency supplies are here. Raise your hood and trunk lid to denote "Help Needed"

6. If you are POSITIVE of the route to help, and must leave your vehicle, leave a note for rescuers as to when you left and the direction you are taking.

7. If you have water — DRINK IT. Do not ration it.

8. If water is limited — KEEP YOUR MOUTH SHUT. Do not talk, do not eat, do not smoke, do not drink alcohol, do not take salt.

9. Do not sit or lie DIRECTLY on the ground. It may be 30 degrees or more hotter than the air.

10. A roadway is a sign of civilization. IF YOU FIND A ROAD, STAY ON IT.

The Desert Southwest is characterized by brilliant sunshine, a wide temperature range, sparse vegetation, a scarcity of water, a high rate of evaporation and low annual rainfall.

Travel in the desert can be an interesting and enjoyable experience or it can be a fatal or near fatal nightmare. The contents of this manual can give only a few of the details necessary for full enjoyment of our desert out-of-doors.

If you think you are lost, do not panic. Sit down for a while, survey the area and take stock of the situation. Try to remember how long it has been since you knew where you were. Decide on a course of action. It may be best to stay right where you are and let your companions or rescuers look for you. This is especially true if there is water and fuel nearby or if there is some means of shelter. Once you decide to remain, make a fire — a smoky one for daytime and a bright one for the night. Other signals may be used, but fire is by far the best.

REMEMBER, MOVE WITH A PURPOSE, NEVER START OUT AND WANDER AIMLESSLY.

Walking: There are special rules and techniques for walking in the desert. By walking slowly and resting about 10 minutes per hour a man in good physical condition can cover about 12-18 miles per day — less after he becomes fatigued or lacks sufficient water or food. On the hot desert it is best to travel early morning or late evening, spending mid-day in whatever shade may be available. In walking, pick the easiest and safest way. Go around obstacles, not over them. Instead of going up or down steep slopes, zigzag to prevent undue exertion. Go around gullies and canyons instead of through them. When walking with companions, adjust the rate to the slowest man. Keep together but allow about 10 feet between members.

At rest stops, if you can sit down in the shade and prop your feet up, remove your shoes and change socks, or straighten out the ones you are wearing. If the ground is too hot to sit on, no shade is available, and you cannot raise your feet, do not remove your shoes as you may not be able to get them back onto swollen feet.

Automobile Driving: Cross country driving or driving on little used roads is hazardous, but can be done successfully if a few simple rules are followed. Move slowly. Do not attempt to negotiate washes without first checking the footing and the clearances. High centers may rupture the oil pan. Overhang may cause the driving wheels to become suspended above the ground. Do not spin wheels in an attempt to gain motion, but apply power very slowly to prevent wheel spin and subsequent digging in. When driving in sand, traction can be increased by partially deflating tires. Start, stop and turn gradually, as sudden motions cause wheels to dig in. There are certain tool and equipment requirements if you intend to drive off the main roads: a shovel, a pick-mattock, a tow chain or cable, at least 50 feet of strong tow rope, tire pump, axe, water cans, gas cans, and of course, your regular spare parts and auto tools.

Clothing: For the desert, light-weight and light colored clothing which covers the whole body is best. Long trousers and long sleeves protect from the sun, help to prevent dehydration and protect against insects, abrasions and lacerations by rocks and brush. Headgear should provide all-around shade as well as eye shade.

Survival Kit: Items that should be carried on the individual are: a sharp knife, a signal mirror, a map of the area, thirty or more feet of nylon string, canteen, matches, a snake bite kit, a firearm and ammunition, and other items that may be useful. Consider carrying your gear in a small rucksack or pack over your shoulders. Weight carried in this manner is less tiring than if carried in pockets or hung on the belt. The pack can be used to sit upon. It also affords a safer method of carrying items, such as the belt knife, hatchet, etc., which may lend to the chances of injury in case of a fall.

Health Hazards: Thought must be given to protecting your health and well-being, and the prevention of fatigue and injury: first, because medical assistance will be some distance away; second, because conditions are usually different and distinct from your everyday living. The desert is a usually healthy environment due to dryness, the lack of human and animal wastes, and the sterilizing effect of the hot sun. Therefore, your immediate bodily needs will be your first consideration.

If you are walking or active, rest 10 minutes each hour. Drink plenty of water, especially early in the morning while the temperature is still low.

While in the desert, wear sun glasses to protect your eyes from glare. Even though the glare does not seem to bother you, it will impair your distant vision and will retard your adaptation to night conditions. If you have no glasses make an eyeshade by slitting a piece of paper, cardboard or cloth. Applying charcoal or soot around the eyes is also beneficial.

In a survival situation everything that you do, each motion that you make, and each step you take must be preceded by the thought: am I safe in doing this?

Keep your clothing on, including shirt and hat. Clothing helps ration your sweat by slowing the evaporation rate and prolonging the cooling effect. It also keeps out the hot desert air and reflects the heat of the sun.

Rationing water at high temperatures is actually inviting disaster because small amounts will not prevent dehydration. Loss of efficiency and collapse always follows dehydration. It is the water in your body that maintains your life, not the water in your canteen.

Keep the mouth shut and breathe through the nose to reduce water loss and drying of mucous membranes. Avoid conversation for the same reason. If possible, cover lips with grease or oil. Alcohol in any form is to be avoided as it will accelerate dehydration. Consider alcohol as food and not as water since additional water is required to assimilate the alcohol. For the same reason, food intake should be kept to a minimum if sufficient water is not available.

Carrying Water: When planning to travel, give your water supply extra thought. Do not carry water in glass containers as these may break. Metal insulated containers are good, but heavy. Carry some water in gallon or half-gallon plastic containers similar to those containing bleach. They are unbreakable, light-weight and carrying several will assure a water supply if one is damaged.

Finding Water in the Desert: If you are near water it is best to remain there and prepare signals for your rescuers. If no water is immediately available look for it, following these leads:

Watch for desert trails — following them may lead to water or civilization, particularly if several such trails join and point toward a specific location.

Flocks of birds will circle over water holes. Listen for their chirping in the morning and evening, and you may be able to locate their watering spot. Quail move toward water in the late afternoon and away in the morning. Doves flock toward watering spots morning and evening. Also look for indications of animals as they tend to feed near water.

Look for plants which grow only where there is water: cottonwoods, sycamores, willows, hackberry, saltcedar, cattails and arrow weed. You may have to dig to find this water. Also keep on the lookout for windmills and water tanks built by ranchers. If cactus fruits are ripe, eat a lot of them to help prevent dehydration.

Methods of Purifying Water: Dirty water should be filtered through several layers of cloth or allowed to settle. This does not purify the water even though it may look clean. Purification to kill germs must be done by one of the following methods:

1. Water purification tablets are the easiest to use. Get them from the drug store and follow the directions on the label. Let stand for thirty minutes.

2. Tincture of Iodine: add three drops per quart of clear water, double for cloudy water. Let stand for thirty minutes.

3. Boiling for 3 to 5 minutes will purify most water.

Food: You must have water to survive, but you can go without food for a few days without harmful effects. In fact, if water is not available, do not eat, as food will only increase your need for water. The important thing about locating food in a survival situation is to know what foods are available in the particular invironment and how to obtain them. Hawks soaring overhead may mean water is nearby. Game will be found around water holes and areas that have heavy brush growth.

Edible Wildlife: Almost every animal, reptile and insect is edible. Learn how to prepare the various things that would be available to you in a survival situation. Avoid any small mammal which appears to be sick. Some animals have scent glands which must be removed before cooking. Do not allow the animal hair to come in contact with the flesh as it will give the meat a disagreeable taste.

1. Jack Rabbit: A hare, with long ears and legs, sandy color. Grubs are often found in the hide or flesh but these do not affect the food value.

2. Cottontail Rabbit: Small, pale gray with white tail. Active in the early morning and late evening.

3. Javelina: Dark gray-black, weighing 30-50 pounds with strong tusks. Has scent glands on the back, over the hind legs. May be dangerous if cornered or wounded.

4. Mourning Dove: Year-round resident, usually found near habitation and water.

5. Gambel's Quail, Scaled Quail, Mearn's Quail: The Gambel's is of primary importance in desert and semi-arid areas.

6. Snakes: Most snakes are edible. Rattlesnake is especially good.

7. Desert Tortoise.

Edible Plants: The main desert edibles are the fruits of the cacti and legumes. All cactus fruits are safe to eat. In the summer the fleshy and thin-walled ripe fruits can be singed over a fire to remove spines. Then they can be peeled and eaten. Old cactus fruits contain seeds which can be pounded between two stones into a powder and eaten, or mixed with water into a gruel. New, young pads of the prickly pear can be singed, peeled and boiled.

The legumes are the bean bearing plants. The main ones are the mesquite, the palo verde, the ironwood and the catclaw. All are small trees with fern-like leaves. All have bean pods which when green and tender can be boiled and eaten. Dry, mature beans, like cactus seeds, are too hard to chew and must be cooked.

In a survival situation, where the use of strange plants for food is indicated, follow these rules: Avoid plants with milky sap. Avoid all red beans. If possible, boil plants which are questionable. Test a cooked plant by holding a small quantity in the mouth for a few moments. If the taste is disagreeable, do not eat it.

Fires and Cooking: Clear an area about 15 feet across, dig a pit or arrange rocks to contain the fire. Make a starting fire of dry grass, small twigs, shavings, under-bark of cottonwoods, etc. Place larger twigs — about pencil size — on top. Have heavier material ready to add, using the small pieces first. Place them on the fire in a "tepee" fashion to prevent smothering your starting fire and aid in the formation of an up-draft. After the fire is burning well, continue to use the tepee method for boiling but criss-cross fuel for forming coals for frying or broiling.

Start your fire with a lighter, matches, or a hand lens. Remember, do not use up your water-proofed matches unless your return from the field is a guaranteed fact. Here are some hints for expeditious fire building.

Drying matches: Damp wooden matches can be dried by stroking 20 to 30 times through the dry hair at the side of the head. Be careful not to knock off the chemical head of very wet matches at the start of the procedure.

Tinder: (All of these must be dry.) Under-bark of the cottonwood, cedar bark, dead goldenrod tops, cattail floss, charred cloth, bird nests, mouse nests, or any readily flammable material shredded into fine fibers.

Fuzz-stick: Cut slivers into soft wood sticks and arrange them tepee fashion with the separated ends downward.

Quick, hot fires: Cottonwood, cactus skeletons, creosote-bush, aspen, tamarisk, cedar, pine, and spruce.

Long-lasting fires: Mesquite, ironwood, black jack, sage, and oak.

REMEMBER, YOU WANT FLAME FOR HEAT, EMBERS FOR COOKING, AND FOR SIGNALS YOU NEED SMOKE IN THE DAYTIME AND BRIGHT FIRES AT NIGHT. BE SURE TO EXTINGUISH YOUR FIRE BEFORE LEAVING IT!

Poisonous Creatures: There is probably more said and less truth about poisonous creatures than any other subject. These animals and insects are for the most part shy, or due to their nature, not often seen. Learn the facts about these creatures and you will see that they are not to be feared but only respected.

Snakes: There are many types of snakes in the southwest but only rattlesnakes and coral snakes are poisonous. Snakes hibernate during the colder months, but will start appearing with the warming trend, sometimes in early February. During the spring and fall months they may be found out in the daytime, but during the summer months they will generally be found out during the night, due to the fact that they cannot stand excessive heat.

Rattlesnakes: These are easily identified by the sandy color, the broad arrow-shaped head, blunt tipped-up nose, and rattles on the tail. Look for them mostly where food, water, and protection is available — around abandoned structures, irrigation ditches, water holes, brush and rock piles. They do not always give warning by rattling, nor do they always strike if one is close. If travelling in areas where rattlers are, wear protective footgear and watch where you put your hands and feet.

Arizona Coral Snake: A small snake, rarely over 20 inches long with small blunt, black head and tapering tail. Wide red and black bands are separated by narrower yellow bands and all completely encircle the body. They are noctunal and live under objects, in burrows, and are shy and timid. Corals bite and chew rather than strike, but due to the very small mouth they are unable to bite any but the smallest extremities.

Treatment of Poisonous Snakebite: If bitten, try to capture the snake as identification will aid in specific medical treatment.

1. KEEP THE VICTIM QUIET AND SEEK MEDICAL HELP.

2. If the "cut and suck" method is deemed necessary, follow the instructions with the snake bite kit. In any event, step 1 above, is very important.

Poisonous Insects and Spiders: The potentially lethal species in this area are the scorpion and the black widow spider.

Prevention and Treatment: In places where venomous species are expected, inspect all clothing and bedding before use, especially items that have been on or near the ground. If bitten (stung), get to a doctor, especially if the victim is a child, is elderly, has a bad heart, or has been bitten several times or on the main part of the body.

What to do
When Lost in the Woods

You might think food, water, proper clothing, or even being attacked by a wild animal, are the most important things with which you had better concern yourself if you are lost in the wilderness.

However, all of the above are secondary or even immaterial if you do not exercise calmness and keep a clear head. If you allow yourself to panic then, indeed, you are lost and will probably only be found by accident. Just because you cannot see a trail or a familiar sight does not mean you cannot find your way back. Understandably, this situation can instill fear but, above all, do not give in to it.

If you find yourself in this situation, do not wander about. Rather, sit down, calm yourself and very carefully try to run through in your mind the events that led up to your getting lost. Instead of letting your feet do the work, use a clear mind.

If you fail to figure out what went wrong and you still have plenty of daylight left, and want to travel slowly, then do so. Make sure, however, that if you had been climbing, you now only travel downhill.

If you come to a stream, do not ever leave it unless, of course, you have found your way. A stream can almost always supply you with water and food, and usually leads to civilization, as well.

Keep a very close eye on the daylight you have left and remember it gets dark earlier on the backside of a mountain away from the sun. If your daylight will soon be gone and you are still lost, you should immediately find a place to camp overnight. Gather whatever rocks or stones are available, place them in a circle to make a place for a safe fire, and gather some wood. You should have a fire burning by dark. Also by the time it's dark, you should have eaten if you have food. You must know where everything in your camp is by then.

If you cannot build a fire because you have no dry

firewood, and you do not have a blanket or bedroll, then cover yourself with sticks and leaves to escape the cold and wind; it works.

If you are injured and cannot travel, then a signal fire is your best bet, of course, using enough common sense not to start a forest fire. A very smoky fire by day and a bright fire at night has the best chance of bringing results.

You can now see how important a fishing line, compass, map, matches and a good knife are in a situation like this, as well as the rest of the supplies that are listed elsewhere in this book. You must always enter the woods prepared, even for the possibility of getting lost.

A situation such as this, before you turn in for the night, may seem hopeless, but can take on a brighter outlook in the morning when again your head is clear.

At the risk of repeating myself, all of the information I have given you so far is useless if you are not going to stay calm and use your head. It has been proven over and over that a clear head will get you out.

What to Wear for Mountain Hiking

In the "Desert Survival" chapter in this book are hints on proper dress for the desert, but mountain dress has a different application. Mountain dress has its variables for lower rolling hills or higher rugged peaks.

LOWER ROLLING HILLS

In these gentle areas, one can use with great comfort the lightweight hiking boots that are popular today. It's not too likely you will need extreme support for lower elevations. Most of these hikes are one-day outings or shorter, so a heavy backpack need not be carried. Lightweight boots will not support a heavy pack.

Hiking shorts or denim pants work well here, as it is not likely to be cold. I prefer long sleeves and a hat to prevent sunburn. A day pack works well on shorter hikes of this nature. Sweat shirt and raingear are a must.

HIGHER RUGGED PEAKS

In this kind of hiking one must have a very rugged hiking boot, not only for traction, but also the ever-present need for good support. Some hikers even buy their boots a half size too large, making room for two pair of socks for more comfort. If you do not buy waterproof boots, then at least spray them with products available to treat them to repel water. These kinds of boots also will support a heavy pack as well as provide comfort.

Again, denim jeans wear well but do not provide much warmth in extreme cold. If you do not wear them hiking, then you might consider carrying in your backpack warmer pants and longjohns for the other conditions. T-shirts are most comfortable under your outer shirts. As you notice, I said "shirts." I do find wearing a couple of shirts instead of one heavy one makes it easier to adjust one's temperature by wearing only what is needed instead of too much or too little.

A warm hat, scarf and mittens should also be carried on these hikes. On mountain hiking, a backpack is needed to carry all necessary supplies. Have the people where you buy your backpack spend some time to insure a proper fit. A backpack is like a boot. It must fit.

Although maybe not worn during hiking, a heavy jacket can be quite an asset when camping or just resting for a while. It is better to be prepared for the worst than to be caught without.

Index

Outdoor books from Golden West

Outdoor enthusiasts welcome this useful, detailed guide to plants, animals, rocks, minerals, geologic history, natural environments, landforms, resources, national forests and outdoor survival. Maps, photos, drawings, charts, index. *Arizona Outdoor Guide* by Ernest E. Snyder (126 pages)...$5.95

Fun on the Verde! Guide to Arizona's Verde River—and its tributaries—section by section! Great for boaters, campers, hikers, tubers, naturalists. Includes types of water to be encountered, surrounding terrain, wildlife. Plus camping and boating advice, whitewater ratings, maps, photos, index. *Verde River Recreation Guide* by Jim Slingluff (176 pages)...$5.95

Enjoy the thrill of discovery! Visit prehistoric ruins and historic battlegrounds! Discover fossil beds, arrowheads, rock crystals and semiprecious stones! Bring your camera! *Discover Arizona!* by Rick Harris (112 pages) . . . $5.00

A guide to the how and why of prehistoric events, the ruins of ancient civilizations in Arizona and their artifacts. Complete with photographs, maps, charts and index.
Prehistoric Arizona
by Dr. Ernest E. Snyder (128 pages)...$5.00

ORDER BLANK

Golden West Publishers

4113 N. Longview Ave.   •   Phoenix, AZ 85014

602-265-4392 • **1-800-658-5830** • FAX 602-279-6901

Number of Copies	TITLE	Per Copy	AMOUNT
	Arizona Adventure	5.95	
	Arizona Cook Book	5.00	
	Arizona—Off the Beaten Path	5.95	
	Arizona Outdoor Guide	5.95	
	Chili-Lovers' Cook Book	5.00	
	Cowboy Cartoon Cookbook	5.95	
	Cowboy Slang	5.95	
	Discover Arizona	5.00	
	Easy Recipes for Wild Game & Fish	6.95	
	Explore Arizona	5.95	
	Ghost Towns in Arizona	5.95	
	Hiking Arizona	5.95	
	Prehistoric Arizona	5.00	
	Quest for the Dutchman's Gold	6.95	
	Snakes and Other Reptiles of the SW	6.95	
	Verde River Recreation Guide	5.95	
	Wild West Characters	5.95	
Add $1.50 to total order for shipping & handling			$1.50

☐ My Check or Money Order Enclosed. . . . . $ —————

☐ Master Card   ☐ VISA

Acct. No.   Exp. Date

Signature

Name

Address

City/State/Zip

Master Card and VISA Orders Accepted ($20 Minimum)
This order blank may be photo-copied.

Hiking AZ